RAISING UNCOMMON K!DS

12 BIBLICAL TRAITS YOU NEED TO RAISE SELFLESS KIDS

SAMI CONE

BakerBooks

a division of Baker Publishing Group
Grand Rapids, Michigan

Published by Baker Books
a division of Baker Publishing Group
P.O. Box 6287, Grand Rapids, MI 49516-6287
www.bakerbooks.com

Printed in the United States of America

Library of Congress Cataloging-in-Publication Data
Cone, Sami, 1975–
    Raising uncommon kids : 12 biblical traits you need to raise selfless kids / Sami Cone.
        pages cm
    Includes bibliographical references.
    ISBN 978-0-8010-1878-7 (pbk.)
    1. Parenting—Religious aspects—Christianity. 2. Child rearing—Religious aspects—Christianity. 3. Parent and child—Religious aspects—Christianity. I. Title.
    BV4529.C598 2016
    248.8′45—dc23   2015034037

Published in association with the literary agency D.C. Jacobson & Associates, an Author Management Company, www.dcjacobson.com.

In keeping with biblical principles of creation stewardship, Baker Publishing Group advocates the responsible use of our natural resources. As a member of the Green Press Initiative, our company uses recycled paper when possible. The text paper of this book is composed in part of post-consumer waste.

16   17   18   19   20   21   22   7   6   5   4   3   2   1

"Sami Cone is a remarkable young woman with the ability to look way beyond her life experiences and determine what it takes to raise healthy, responsible, God-loving children. In *Raising Uncommon Kids*, she gives readers practical information for the 'hows' all parents want to know, such as 'How do we teach our children to love their siblings?' I'm thankful for women like Sami who are dedicated to teaching our next generation that 'things' don't matter—others do."

Chrys Howard, *Duck Dynasty*

"If you want to see your kids grow up to be men and women of great character, then this book is a must-have for you. It's an extraordinary tool that will give you some practical tips for raising selfless kids in an it's-all-about-me generation."

Pete Wilson, senior pastor of Cross Point Church and bestselling author of *Plan B*

"In her book *Raising Uncommon Kids*, Sami Cone shows us how to shepherd the hearts of our children with biblical wisdom and contemporary courage. This book is packed with personal stories and creative ideas your family will love. Get ready to experience more of Jesus in your everyday life and lead your kids closer to the heart of God."

Renee Swope, bestselling author of *A Confident Heart* and cohost of *Everyday Life with Lysa & Renee* on Proverbs 31 Ministries Radio

"Sami Cone is such a smart woman and mother. Her refreshing ideas on raising uncommon kids gave me hope in the moment and encouragement for the future. This book is a must-have for any parent who cares enough to give their kids every opportunity to become successful adults."

Jaci Velasquez, Grammy-nominated and Dove Award–winning vocalist

"Warning: be prepared to ditch the parenting status quo! If you're looking for a spiritually sound and practical guide to take your family to the next level, look no further. Sami Cone's transparent and practical style is a breath of fresh air in the parenting space. I pride myself in being wildly intentional, and now it's your turn—grab this book!"

Carrie Wilkerson, bestselling author of *The Barefoot Executive*, international speaker, and award-winning podcaster

"Raising kids who love God and love others is the greatest blessing you can receive as a parent. But that blessing comes as a result of a lot of hard work and discipline to model the virtues and character traits of Christ in your home. Remember, more is caught than taught by our kids! In *Raising Uncommon Kids*, Sami unpacks the twelve godly characteristics that will challenge and inspire you to walk closer with Jesus so you can raise kids who will change the world for Christ in their generation."

Tom and Donna Mullins, founders of Christ Fellowship and Place of Hope

"I love Sami, and not just because she can light up a room when she enters but because she can make me laugh like nobody's business. Not only is she an amazing woman of God, but she is also an intentional wife and mother. Her book *Raising Uncommon Kids* is refreshing, inspiring, and honest. She shoots straight from the heart. I am excited to see how her book empowers moms to find the joy in finishing well with one of the most important titles we could ever have: mother."

Shelene Bryan, author of *Love, Skip, Jump* and founder of Skip1.org

"Sami and her family have been great friends of ours, and I am so happy she has shared her life lessons! My husband and I have asked Sami and Rick on many occasions how they have raised such respectful and kind children. The answers were truthful, powerful, and Christ-centered. I cannot wait for the rest of the world to hear these ideas as well! Thank you, Sami, for helping all of us raise 'uncommon kids'!"

Kelly Sutton, TV host and entertainment journalist

To my husband and parenting partner, Ricky, who made it possible for me to be a mother in the first place. I love you forever and for always.

And to our own uncommon kids, Kariss Nevaeh and Britton Jerick. Thank you for allowing me to see the world through your eyes. You two are the best mirror a mom could ask for!

CONTENTS

INTRODUCTION

Hello, Pot, Meet Kettle—
Your Mirror Image

I educate over a million people each day through television, radio, and my blog, yet a few years ago, I couldn't seem to figure out how to teach my own kids one of the most important qualities they could have: compassion.

The genesis of this book was in a heart's cry to God one night after my daughter had been, in my opinion, exceedingly selfish. Before sending her off to bed, I prayed desperately, "God, help me show Kariss what it truly means to put the needs of others ahead of her own wants."

Then, as my daughter lay in bed, I found myself telling a tale to her that only God could have planted in my head. It was the perfect little story that not only related to her own world, but somehow made the plight of children around the world more tangible to her.

Of course, it starred her as the main character, so it captured her attention right away. But more important, I saw a twinkle in her eye and a light go on in her head that I had never seen before.

I knew God had shared something special with me and from that moment forward, I felt a strong pull to share it so others could spark the same flame in their own children.

Still, I was surprised when almost two years later, a book agent captured the same vision I so desperately wanted to share with others.

But then he suggested, "Instead of making this a children's fable, why not direct it toward parents going through the same struggles with their children you are?"

Honestly, it caught me off guard.

After all, this wasn't about me and my character, but instead about my daughter's selfishness and her need to change.

And then it hit me. Where had she learned this behavior? Where had she learned it was okay to want every McDonald's Happy Meal toy in a series? Where had she learned it was fine to have a room full of stuff, yet want more? Where had she learned to expect presents for every holiday (including half-birthdays)?

She learned it from me.

If I wanted my daughter to change, I realized, the change had to start with me.

It dawned on me that I didn't need to write a parenting book so much as I needed to write a book to people who happen to have kids who will watch, study, and emulate them—which pretty much describes every parent.

In *Boundaries with Kids* by Henry Cloud and John Townsend, I read that we parents have three main avenues of influence over our children: teaching, modeling, and internalizing. Teaching involves helping your children identify experiences and apply your instruction to new situations. Modeling goes a step further to where your children learn directly from watching how you operate and treat others, regardless of whether or not you intend to teach them something. Helping your children to internalize equips them to take their positive experiences and traits and make them a part of their everyday reality.[1]

You may be looking for a quick fix for your kids; I'm here to coach you in paying a little less attention to their behavior and spending a little more time evaluating your own.

It's been said that we rarely see an accurate picture of what the mirror reflects back to us, and I think that statement is even more accurate with how we see our kids. While others may see them as wonderful and kind, we may only be aware of what annoys us if we are mainly seeing ourselves in them. Likewise, some of what we think is cute about our own children could drive others nuts.

> *I'm here to coach you in paying a little less attention to your kids' behavior and spending a little more time evaluating your own.*

So where better to look for the traits we need to embrace than the Bible?

Ever since my first time reading Colossians 3:12–17, I've felt drawn to the passage.

> Therefore, as God's chosen people, holy and dearly loved, clothe yourselves with compassion, kindness, humility, gentleness and patience. Bear with each other and forgive one another if any of you has a grievance against someone. Forgive as the Lord forgave you. And over all these virtues put on love, which binds them all together in perfect unity.
>
> Let the peace of Christ rule in your hearts, since as members of one body you were called to peace. And be thankful. Let the message of Christ dwell among you richly as you teach and admonish one another with all wisdom through psalms, hymns, and songs from the Spirit, singing to God with gratitude in your hearts. And whatever you do, whether in word or deed, do it all in the name of the Lord Jesus, giving thanks to God the Father through him.

What particularly strikes me is that verse 14 says "binds them all together in perfect unity" (or "harmony," as it states in the NLT).

It drives home a message that, while each of the characteristics outlined in these verses is important, they are best when combined.

It reminds me of another favorite Scripture passage of mine, 2 Peter 1:5–8.

> For this very reason, make every effort to add to your faith goodness; and to goodness, knowledge; and to knowledge, self-control; and to self-control, perseverance; and to perseverance, godliness; and to godliness, mutual affection; and to mutual affection, love. For if you possess these qualities in increasing measure, they will keep you from being ineffective and unproductive in your knowledge of our Lord Jesus Christ.

Not only does it embody the same principle of embracing pivotal characteristics of our faith incrementally, but did you catch verse 8? "If you possess these qualities in increasing measure, they will keep you from being ineffective and unproductive in your knowledge of our Lord Jesus Christ."

It's like it was written just for parents!

When I read this for the first time, I thought, "Jesus totally gets me!" I wasn't as worried about being effective and productive for Christ as I was about trying to make sure I wasn't being ineffective or unproductive! He wasn't setting the bar low; he was meeting me where I was in my own parenting journey.

After all, how many days is your only goal to survive until dinner (especially when you're parenting toddlers)?

I remember younger moms asking me when my kids said their first words, took their first steps, or ate their first solid food. Do you want to know what my brilliant answer was as the mom of two kids just nineteen months apart? "I'm sure I wrote it down somewhere, but for now my goal is just to keep them breathing."

Just as I was in the midst of figuring out how to keep my children alive and well, God laid out a clear road map in these verses to guide us as we guide our children.

So with Colossians 3:12–17 as my guide, I've taken twelve parenting dilemmas I have personally faced and framed them into twelve characteristics God calls us to emulate. I didn't always tackle them the way I wish I had, but I have learned from each scenario, and that's what I'd like to share with you in the coming pages.

This book has three sections. In each section, you'll find four unique characteristics and focuses that not only build on each other but are built from within your four walls and eventually out into the world. You will learn how to love from the One who loved us first and then take that love to anyone and everyone you encounter in your life.

The breakdown looks like this:

Section One: Your Heart at Home

1. *Love* (focus: God)
2. *Harmony* (focus: Character of the Home)
3. *Gentleness* (focus: Parent to Child)
4. *Bearing With* (focus: Child to Child/Siblings)

Section Two: Your Attitude toward Others

5. *Forgiveness* (focus: Extended Family)
6. *Wisdom* (focus: School)
7. *Patience* (focus: Church/Community Group)
8. *Kindness* (focus: Neighbor/Neighborhood)

Section Three: Your Influence in the World

9. *Gratitude* (focus: City)
10. *Peace* (focus: State)
11. *Humility* (focus: Country)
12. *Compassion* (focus: World)

At the end of every chapter, I've listed some practical applications for you to take these ideas from the pages to the street.

You can focus on one character trait a month, or you can devour them all in one sitting. Ultimately, it's up to you.

Just promise me one thing: act on what you read. Because what good is it if knowledge goes in but action doesn't come out as a result?

So don't just strive to have kids "like everyone else." In fact, your goal should be to have kids unlike others. Go against the grain. Raise uncommon kids.

YOUR HEART AT HOME

I love a good deal.

In fact, I am rather well known for my deal-finding strategies and savvy saving advice. So it should come as no surprise to learn that from a young age, my kids were known to utter phrases like, "Do we have a coupon for that, Mommy?"

To this day, before my kids ask me to buy something, I will often hear them telling each other, "You have to wait until it goes on sale!"

But I think the ultimate kicker was when I heard my (at the time) two-year-old daughter tell my mother-in-law, "Nani, you can get that much cheaper at Walmart."

Frankly, I wasn't sure whether to laugh or cry.

Did I sit down daily and educate my two toddlers on how to save money by stacking coupons with store sales?

Of course not.

But at the time, we had just hit rock bottom financially due to the economic crash. We went from two modest incomes to one and had to sell a car just to make ends meet. This meant that

I accomplished all of our shopping and daily activities with a double stroller.

Can you just picture it? Me walking to the bank, grocery store, bookstore, and yes, even Walmart with my two kids under two in a double stroller. Not only did we have to be picky about our prices, but we had to plan each trip extremely carefully because we could only buy what would fit in the basket beneath our double stroller.

In the midst of those circumstances, I often threw myself a mini pity party. Yet as I reflect back on that eighteen-month stint, I can honestly say it was one of the sweetest periods of our lives. We learned to focus on what was truly important and were reminded that relationships remained our most prized possessions.

During those months when I felt I wasn't providing adequately for my kids, I was actually doing the best thing we can do as parents: put what we say into practice.

Which is why I'm writing this book: to tell you something you probably already know yet most of us overlook in the throes of day-to-day parenting.

The key to raising uncommon kids may surprise you: it starts with you. Your influence will impact your kids far more than your instruction.

In these first four chapters, we'll start building the foundation necessary for raising selfless kids in a self-centered world from within the four walls of your home—by examining the characteristics of love, harmony, gentleness, and bearing with one another.

1

LOVE

Above All Else

We want more.

We want more stuff. We want more "likes" on Facebook. We want more friends. We want more vacation time. And yes, we want more for our kids.

But how can we realistically raise compassionate kids content with less when they're constantly being told more is better?

It starts with us.

Before we can raise uncommon kids, we have to be uncommon ourselves. That means everything you've heard about living in the world but not being of it—and then some.

It's not wrong to want more for your kids, depending on what you want more of.

Every day, I pray for more wisdom, more kindness, more generosity, more joy, more contentment, and yes, more compassion within my children.

Does this mean we ought to strip ourselves and our kids of every creature comfort? Of course not. But it does mean we need to take a harder, more evaluative look at who we are, what we do, what we have, and why we have it.

While a child's behavior is not always a direct representation of their parent's influence, a parent's influence should have a direct impact on the behavior of their child.

> *Before we can raise uncommon kids, we have to be uncommon ourselves.*

Don't lose heart! Though this may seem daunting initially, you should instead see it as an immediate and effective way to start influencing the legacy you will leave with your children.

The Bible contains 393 verses that talk about love, including Colossians 3:14, which reminds us, "Above all, clothe yourselves with love" (NLT). While that verse may make it seem as though love ought to be the final characteristic we study, I'd argue it should be the first. Without love, the rest of what we will discuss will be meaningless.

Think of the characteristics in the chapters of this book as blocks in a pyramid, each one building upon the other. All are necessary to complete the pyramid, but it's first important to start with a firm and solid foundation.

And where do we learn about love? From the very first father who ever was: our heavenly Father. After all, 1 John 4:8 says, "God is love." If we truly want to show our kids love, we must first understand the most pure and perfect love there is. Before we can understand that, we need to first be willing recipients of such love. For that, we can go only to God.

My Unique Religious Road

Some of you may be thinking, *I already know God and his love. Can we just skip to the part where we fix my selfish kids?*

If there's one thing I've learned in my forty years of life, it's that no one experiences God quite the same way. I've come to understand that even those of you who grew up going to church, or at least believing in God, have a journey unlike anyone else's.

I grew up in what you could call a "religiously confused" home. My father is Jewish, and my mother grew up Church of England (Anglican). Though my parents divorced when I was seven, the years we did spend under the same roof were interesting from a religious standpoint.

> *A parent's influence should have a direct impact on the behavior of their child.*

While my parents were not what I'd call very religious, neither did they seem to want to give in to the other. For example, during the winter season, we'd pick up a short Christmas tree and call it a "Hanukkah bush." We also lit the menorah each night during Hanukkah, but I didn't get presents like Jewish children traditionally would.

Friends at school thought I was so lucky because I got to celebrate double holidays, but what they didn't know was that it didn't mean double presents.

While we never went to church or synagogue while my parents were married, things changed after their divorce.

During my middle school years, my mom became an evangelical Christian. But having grown up in middle-class, suburban Chicago up until that point, I'd witnessed a lot of religious hypocrisy firsthand among my friends' families. As a result, I wasn't too keen on joining in, regardless of what the religion was called.

I distinctly remember telling my mom I was considering becoming Jewish when she asked me to go to church. Likewise, I'd tell my father I was considering becoming Christian anytime the topic of a bat mitzvah came up.

The Religious Tides Change

It was during the middle school years, however, that two of my best friends invited me to a summer church camp. I'd never been to a sleep-away camp to know what I was getting into, but I'm sure it was pretty much like what you're imagining in your head right now: older cabins, high school counselors, plenty of outdoor activities, and a plethora of sleeping bags.

In fact, so many sleeping bag packs had been dumped into a pile upon arrival (á la the young Lindsay Lohan version of *The Parent Trap*), that at first I could not find mine. Then as I quietly watched other campers reclaim their possessions and the pile got smaller, my pack was nowhere in sight.

This might not seem like a huge deal upon first glance, but what I didn't mention was that inside my sleeping bag, I'd rolled up my prized "cutie blankie" and my favorite Pound Puppies stuffed animal. I'd had "cutie" since I was a baby, and I'd rather have eaten any bug they could throw my way than imagine life without my blanket.

I'm pretty sure that's when the sobbing started.

The rest of my memory from that night is a bit hazy, but I believe it involved a trip to the camp director's office to call my mom and beg to go home. They must have convinced my mom that all would be okay, because I didn't get back on the bus to go home. Instead I spent the night on top of a cold, hard bunk in a borrowed sleeping bag.

Suffice it to say, I didn't exactly sleep well that night. As I lay stiffly and stared at the ceiling of the old cabin, I made a promise to God. Amid tears I couldn't manage to stop from streaming down my face, I bartered with this higher power I didn't yet fully believe in: I promised if he found my blanket and puppy (honestly, the sleeping bag was the least of my concerns at that point), I'd believe in Jesus.

I thought it was a pretty good deal.

I recognize this isn't the typical path people take in following Christ, but in my middle school–aged heart and mind, it was 100 percent genuine.

Much to my surprise, I eventually did fall asleep that night, and when I awoke it was to my counselor, who was taking me back to the camp director's office. Can you imagine what I discovered once there?

My sleeping bag pack! After I confirmed that my prized possessions were indeed inside, the director explained that a Russian foreign exchange student misunderstood the bag retrieval process after getting off the bus and grabbed my sleeping pack by mistake.

It didn't matter how it had happened. My blanket and puppy had been found. In my mind, God kept his end of the bargain, so I needed to keep mine. And thus, I prayed to accept Jesus. After all, I'm a woman of my word.

One thing that's important to note about my personality back then is that I was an extreme people-pleaser. I also generated much of my self-worth from my accomplishments and believed the only way to receive love was to perform well at whatever I was doing: academics, sports, you name it.

So from that point forward, at least while at camp, I purposed to become the best Christian I could be—and that included memorizing as many Bible verses as possible to win the top award at camp. And that's about as far as my faith went for the remainder of my school years.

Fast-forward to my midtwenties. I'd continued living life as the "good girl," which meant I played with a lot of fire while straddling the line between love and acceptance.

After working at a spring training stadium for a Major League Baseball team for almost a year, I found myself in a predicament that completely rocked my world: not only had I ended up in a relationship with one of the players (something I said I'd never do) but then I discovered he was married.

I could not believe how I'd landed in this place.

I made a phone call to a pastor I'd sold season tickets to and asked if I could come speak with him. Long story short, I was told to "fast and pray" during my lunch hour that week (two words that were very foreign to me at the time) and listen for God to speak to me. When I returned that instruction with a blank stare, he told me to close my office door during my lunch hour, skip eating, and instead sit quietly in reflection.

At the end of that week (April 20, 2000, to be exact), I distinctly heard God say to me, "Whether people like you or dislike you, they will respect you when you live a consistent life for me."

In that instant, the weight of people-pleasing I'd been carrying most of my life instantly lifted off my shoulders. From that moment forward, I dug into not only learning about the Bible, but more important, learning about Jesus and cultivating a relationship with him.

My Husband's Journey

My husband grew up deeply rooted in a church culture. He went to a private Christian school, and even grew up in a neighborhood that was literally planted around the church. Two other sets of relatives lived on that same street, with his nana living just one street over.

To say our worlds differed would be an understatement. One similarity is that he too "stretched his wings" during his college and young-adult years. Though he continued to go to church, he was not walking with God.

Through a series of events, he felt called to move back to Florida from Nashville. He did so begrudgingly, and we met two days later. Five months later we were engaged, and five months after that we were married. Our first child would be due on our one-year wedding anniversary.

So there we had it: two kids from divorced families who met, married, and procreated in just over a year. Now, all of a sudden, we were faced with dealing with our own conceptions of religion, having to decide what we would pass on to our children—and how.

A House Full of Love

What we lacked in knowledge, we made up for in love. While my husband and I came from different spiritual backgrounds, we purposed to root our children in a shared faith that we prayed would one day become real to them.

The irony we realized was that we are called to teach and train our children in the ways of the Lord. But the only way ours would truly come to know what it meant to love the Lord would be to see us model those very teachings, both within and outside our homes.

So we prayed and collaborated on what our spiritual map of faith would look like inside the Cone home. We started by setting certain nonnegotiables:

- We would start each day with devotions.
- We would begin each meal with prayer. In fact, we created a simple prayer covering the essentials that our kids could learn quickly to say before every meal: "Thank you for our family, thank you for our food, bless it to our bodies, Amen."
- We would read either a character-filled or Bible-based story to our children each night.
- We would pray a special prayer over our children right before leaving their bedroom each night, beginning from the time they were born. Because of this, each of our kids had it memorized and could say it aloud with us by the time they

were two, and we still end our prayers with it each night. The prayer is taken directly from Proverbs 6:20–23: "My son, keep your father's command and do not forsake your mother's teaching. Bind them always on your heart, fasten them around your neck. When you walk, they will guide you; when you sleep, they will watch over you, when you wake, they will speak to you. For this command is a lamp, this teaching is a light, and correction and instruction are the way to life."

I can already hear some of you pushing back: "This seems more robotic than genuine love." But let me remind you of one of the most common misconceptions about love: it's not simply a feeling, it's a choice.

If we all waited to love others until we "felt like it," I'd venture to say we would see few acts of love in the world. Much like if we waited until we felt like it to eat healthfully and exercise, we

MENTOR MOMENT
AM I ALWAYS LOVELY?

When we lived in South Florida and attended Christ Fellowship, our pastor (a former football coach) constantly reminded his church family to "suck it up and get tough."

Now, don't mistake that tough exterior for anything other than what it is. He and his wife, Ms. Donna, are some of the kindest, most genuine and compassionate people you would ever want to meet.

In fact, it was starting to get to me at one point when I realized they said they loved me and my family, but they also seemed to equally love another family that had hurt us, and I just couldn't see that family as being very lovable.

I earnestly approached Ms. Donna after church one Saturday night to ask her a serious question. In retrospect, she must have thought I was going to drop a deep, philosophical bomb on her.

wouldn't see many people losing weight. Instead, fitness experts recommend setting a realistic goal and sticking with it every day until (a) it becomes a habit or (b) an internal change takes place that then drives external behavior.

Spiritual Discipline

The same principle about choosing action instead of waiting for a feeling can be applied to spiritual discipline.

There are no requirements for how and/or when we approach God; the important thing is to do it, and do it regularly.

As a morning person, I enjoy starting my day with devotions and journaling. For some of you, that's not possible, so you make time for Bible study before bed. Still others may use a lunch hour to do what I did back in my baseball days: use your allotted work breaks to reconnect with God and recalibrate your thinking.

But instead I just cried out, "How can you possibly love everyone you meet?"

She tilted her head, smiled a gentle smile, and said, "Oh Sami, I didn't always used to be this way. Tom has taught me such a valuable lesson over all these years. There is always at least one good thing you can find about someone; you just focus on that one good thing and love them through the rest."

I have never forgotten those words or that moment. After all, am I always lovely? As much as I'd like to think so, we all know the answer to that question.[1]

Donna Mullins is the wife of Tom Mullins, the founding pastor of Christ Fellowship and the President of EQUIP. She is also the co-founder of Place of Hope, a faith-based, state-licensed child welfare organization in South Florida. She and Tom have a son, Todd, who is married to Julie; a daughter, Noelle; and a grandson, Jefferson.

This is all well and good in theory, but for those of you who are visual learners, I thought it might be helpful to share how my different spiritual disciplines emerge throughout my day.

Here's a sample of my typical routine:

5:30 Wake up and go for a walk while I listen to a podcast from a Christian teacher/pastor I respect and can learn something from and be challenged by.

6:15 Dive in to my devotions and journaling. At a minimum, my morning must-read is *My Utmost for His Highest* by Oswald Chambers. I've been reading from the same copy for so long that it has a layer of Press'n Seal holding the cover together. Depending on the time, I may also read from the *One Year Bible* and then journal.

7:15 Pray with my kids before breakfast, referring to our prayer poster and prayer shield (see more about these later).

8:20 Drive the kids to school and pray over them and their day before I drop them off, asking them for any special requests or concerns about what's coming up that day in class, with friends, or with teachers.

10:30 Try to take a midday break to stand, take a couple of deep breaths, and express gratitude in a quick prayer.

12:30 Before eating lunch, reflect on my day thus far and check in with God to see if I'm truly spending my time where I should on things that are of value.

3:30 While waiting in the school car line, ask God to help me redirect my focus from whatever I've been doing that day to preparing my mind to receive whatever our children are ready to share with me from their day at school.

5:00 When possible, involve our kids in cooking/preparing for dinner, being mindful to listen more than I talk so I model how our heavenly Father wants us to sit at his feet and share what's on our minds.

7:30 Start the bedtime routine—have the kids help choose a book and then read together. (My husband is the best at this. His voices and inflections are far superior to mine!)

8:00 Tuck the kids in bed, pray our special prayer (Prov. 6:20–23), and give lots of hugs and kisses before walking out their door.

10:30 Pray with my husband before going to sleep, reflecting on our day and praying for tomorrow. If we're not too tired at this point, we'll read a section from a book we're working through together or from our 7 *Minute Marriage Solution Bible*.

Other spiritual disciplines we engage in regularly, besides going to church on Sunday, include going to community group once a week, working through Bible studies periodically throughout the year, serving as a family on mission trips, and volunteering in our community.

I never recommend people do exactly what I do, but I hope sharing my routine will challenge you to think about why you do what you do.

Parenting Mirror: Do You See What I See?

Just as you don't want to hide chips and cookies in your pantry and tell your kids they are "only for Mommy," you don't want to confuse your kids by encouraging them in their own spiritual disciplines if you never engage in spiritual disciplines yourself.

While your kids won't always be honest with you, they never seem to fail at spilling the beans when they are with others. This mere fact can terrify most parents, but I experienced a delightful example when Kariss was about six years old.

Every once in a while our children's teachers at church will ask them a series of questions about themselves or us as their parents, typically in the form of a questionnaire that they'd hand to us at the end of service on Mother's Day or Father's Day. Kariss was asked to describe me, and you know what she said? "My mommy loves God."

I guarantee my daughter didn't know that because I told her I loved God; she could say that because she saw I loved God as demonstrated through my daily actions.

But even more important is that my daughter's answer proved she felt loved by me as well, because if she didn't know what it meant to be loved she could never accurately describe love in others.

Now that we've laid a foundation of love, your family should begin to understand not just the source of all love, but why we would in turn want to share that love with others, especially within our own home. Moving toward the uncommon may start with a characteristic, but only by studying and seeking it out in an entirely new way.

❗ Make It Practical

I've now given you a glimpse into my own spiritual disciplines as well as my family's. While every individual and family loves God differently, the overarching point is this: God loves each of us equally and we cannot love others until we grasp that basic, yet life-changing concept.

Once we as parents truly embrace the love of our heavenly Father, we must exhibit that love daily and put it into practice. Only then will our children understand what it means to love with an everlasting love and be able to walk away from the common path and instead run toward the uncommon.

To do this, foundational practices ought to be discussed, adapted, and then put into practice as a family. If you're looking for a baseline from which to start, consider some of the activities listed below that not only work to bring your family together but bring you closer to the love of our Lord.

- *Establish consistent devotions as an individual and as a family.* It doesn't matter so much when you have your personal and family devotions, as long as you make time for this important period of reflection each day.

- *Tithe.* Set aside a set percentage of any money that comes into your home to give away, either to your home church or a nonprofit you and your family feels passionate about.
- *Offer your time.* Give generously of your time and talents on a regular basis.
- *Model worship.* Your kids will never understand what it means to worship until they experience it firsthand. Model worship in your home regularly through speech and song.
- *Create a gratitude journal.* Encourage each member of your family to create and keep a gratitude journal. For little ones, this may be as simple as having them draw a picture every day of something they're grateful for. For tweens and teens, you may want them to use an app on their smartphone to make a daily list of one thing they're grateful for every morning before they start their day and every evening after they return home. In our family, we take time during breakfast and dinner to have everyone share one thing their grateful for and one thing they're praying about, and I keep track of those lists in a shared family notebook.
- *Follow a nighttime prayer routine.* You can read more about ours at http://samicone.com/kids-bedtime-routine-prayer/.

Once we as parents truly embrace the love of our heavenly Father, we must exhibit that love daily and put it into practice.

For more practical tips and guidelines, visit
SamiCone.com/UncommonKids.

2

HARMONY

Lessons Are Caught

I love concrete.

I get energized when I see skyscrapers.

It's safe to say, you could call me a city girl.

My only request when we moved to Nashville from Florida several years ago was that we have a Nashville mailing address. I didn't want to be one of those people who said they lived in the city but actually lived sixty miles away.

Growing up in Chicago and its suburbs, I'd grown accustomed to taking advantage of all an urban area has to offer. To say the least, I was not ready to buy a pair of cowboy boots and live in the country.

Within a year of moving, we'd settled into a multilevel apartment building about twelve miles from downtown, yet safely situated in a family-friendly area of Nashville. I was quite content with my ability to turn left onto the main road and be downtown within minutes and to call the leasing office when any appliances broke down.

But the joy didn't last long.

As typically happens after something new gets old, I began to feel unrest. I started believing the lies: Someone my age should own a home. I needed to "set some roots." I was somehow abusing my small children by raising them in an apartment and not giving them a proper backyard to frolic in anytime they pleased.

Fast-forward two and a half years when we found a short-sale home that offered us everything we thought we wanted in a "forever" home: more living area, individual rooms for our kids, office space, a guest room, a corner lot on a cul-de-sac, and yes, that ever-important fenced-in backyard.

Believe it or not, we closed on that home in less than a month and did imagine ourselves there forever. We let the kids pick out individual paint colors for their bedrooms because it was the first time in their lives they didn't have to share a room. We built a swing set onto our deck. I even planted a small garden (which was no small feat for this city girl).

But you'll never guess what happened. Or maybe you will.

The upstairs area designed almost exclusively for our kids rarely got used. They wanted to be closer to us, so they often slept together downstairs in the guest room. Our son never liked to sleep by himself, so when they did sleep upstairs, he made a pallet to sleep on his sister's floor. They even preferred bringing their toys downstairs and playing with them in closer proximity to us.

So essentially, we basically lived in and spent the majority of our time as a family in a space smaller than our original apartment.

And that yard we thought crucial to our children's development? Turns out my daughter is allergic to grass.

For whatever reason that hadn't been incredibly clear before, the truth was simple: the size of our home didn't matter as much as the harmony—and joy—we experienced together as a family within the space.

Finding Joy and Harmony

Oswald Chambers rocked my world recently as I was reading his classic devotional *My Utmost for His Highest*. Though I've read it daily for years, I find it speaks to me in new ways every time, based on what I'm going through in that moment.

After spending a night paralyzed by negative emotions that I lightly refer to as my "dark pit" (which ended up being diagnosed as clinical depression), I woke up the next morning to discover the title of that day's devotional was "Receiving Yourself in the Fires of Sorrow." In it, Chambers reveals:

> My attitude toward sorrow and difficulty should not be to ask that they be prevented, but to ask that God protect me so that I may remain what He created me to be, in spite of all my fires of sorrow. Our Lord received Himself . . . in the midst of the fire of sorrow. He was saved not from the hour, but out of the hour. . . . If you will receive yourself in the fires of sorrow, God will make you nourishment for other people.[1]

Our mission should not be to prevent difficulty in the lives of our children (or our own lives, for that matter), but instead to model for them how to find joy in the midst of pain and difficulty.

We learned to choose joy instead of chasing it.

It wasn't long after our move that we heard our kids say they actually wanted to move back to our apartment. For us, that cemented the lesson that our joy is not and cannot be rooted in our surroundings or circumstances.

Not wanting to overreact and quickly erase the move, we purposed to redefine our priorities and model what joy looked like in our present circumstance and beyond. We learned to choose joy instead of chasing it. If we were to create harmony in our home, it had to begin with us as individuals and then together as parents.

Harmony in the Home

Harmony in the home has several components, most notably the spiritual, emotional, and physical.

In chapter one, I spoke about the importance of love in setting a spiritual foundation for our families, and I will give more practical ways to demonstrate that to our children in this chapter. But for now I want to dwell on the latter two.

While how we feel should not be based on or dictated by the feelings of others, we would be foolish to believe our own feelings and actions have no bearing on those of our children. The truth is that our children learn more from watching us than we care to admit, both good and bad.

Let's face the hard truth.

- If we don't buy it, they won't play with it.
- If we don't cook it, they won't eat it.

MENTOR MOMENT
WHAT ONLY YOU CAN PROVIDE

As parents, we can often get wrapped up in caring for our kids instead of loving on each other. However, the longer you neglect your marriage "for the sake of the kids," the greater the danger of actually losing it.

In chapter one, I introduced you to Ms. Donna from the church we attended in Florida. An equally loving and impactful woman from that church was Jane Randlett. Ms. Jane was the first woman to teach me the importance of memorizing full chapters of the Bible (instead of simply memorizing stand-alone verses). Just as meaningful was this story she told me about a realization in her marriage regarding the role we play as wives.

As a pastor's wife, it never surprised me that my husband would come into contact with so many people on a daily basis. But what I didn't expect was just how many women he'd encounter. Even after decades of our serving together, even though other women

- If we don't go through the drive-through, they won't expect it.
- If we don't say it, they won't say it.

In essence, your family models and sets the tone of "normal" for your kids.

Scary, isn't it?

In our me-centered culture, our children are used to getting their way. But then again, so are we.

- We yell at cars in front of us whose drivers are going too slow.
- We sigh repeatedly when made to wait more than fifteen minutes in the doctor's office.
- We lose our temper when our kids forget their lunch or homework.

Imagine if instead we took a minute to reframe our thinking and then chose joy in each of those situations.

clearly knew we were married, they'd still approach my husband after service.

Some were well meaning in their encouraging remarks about the message he preached that day or what a good job he was doing in his role there. Others lavished him with gifts ranging from homemade pies to other forms of flattery. In those moments, I was reminded of just how many women would be happy to step in and take my place to meet his needs if I wasn't willing.

If you're so busy with everything and everyone around you to the point where your husband feels neglected, beware. Technically, you can legally hire someone to take care of every physical need you have, except one. If you cannot find time to be intimate with your husband, he might look elsewhere to fill that need. And never forget, how you treat your spouse ultimately sets the tone for how your kids will treat others.[2]

Jane Randlett is a mother of two, grandmother of four, wife of a pastor, lifetime mentor, and former instructor at Liberty University.

- We'd realize perhaps God was protecting us from an accident happening ahead of us on the road and thank him for our safety.
- We'd think of the citizens of third world countries who walk days just to receive vaccines and be grateful for the climate-controlled room we are sitting in.
- We'd think back to our own childhood and remember the kind teacher who reminded us mistakes happen and modeled grace and forgiveness.

If only creating happy kids was as simple as playing the Bobby McFerrin hit song over and over again under their pillows as they slept—"Don't worry, be happy!"

Yet if I've learned one thing since becoming a Christian, it's that happiness and joy are distinctly different; even when we are not happy, we can always choose joy.

We can neither predict nor guarantee our children's happiness, but as we learned in chapter one, we can teach them where the source of harmony and joy begins: with the Lord. A beautiful revelation rests in the fact that once your children experience the joy you discover in the Lord, that joy is contagious.

If I had to sum up this idea in one sentence, it would be this: *Lessons are caught, not taught.* What you do has far more impact on your children than what you say.

Living in Nashville, I'm exposed to more country music than I'd ever care to admit I enjoy. But shortly after moving here, one song in particular stuck out in my mind. Actually, it was the music video depicting country artist Rodney Atkins with his son that made even more of an impact.

In "Watching You," we follow Rodney and his small boy, who is mimicking every move his dad makes, including less-than-desirable gestures during heavy traffic. The chorus echoes, "I've been watching you, Dad, ain't that cool?"

Once the father realizes the impact his every move and word have on his son, you see a 180-degree spin in his behavior, with his son then following in his daddy's footsteps on the farm, on the field, and even in prayer.

It's such a simple yet poignant reflection that each and every move we make has an impact on the minds of our children, which in turn ultimately affects their behavior.

The good news is that we can stop lecturing our children so much in an attempt to cram all our years of valuable experience into their brains; the bad news is that we can't rely on those self-defined brilliant lectures to cram all our years of valuable experience into their brains.

So what's a parent to do?

Create a family mission and vision, and then actually live it out.

Parenting Mirror: Family Mission Statement

You may have heard of businesses creating a mission statement, but have you ever considered doing the same for your family?

I was first introduced to the idea when my kids were young via Patrick Lencioni's book *The 3 Big Questions for a Frantic Family*.[3]

The first two-thirds of the book is told in fable format, detailing the typically busy, overtired, overcommitted family with two kids found in many of our nation's homes today. Throughout the course of the fable, it describes their need for change and what they do to create exactly that for themselves, implementing a strategy the husband had up until that point reserved for his business clients.

The last third of the book breaks down the system for how any family can implement that strategy, complete with templates—my love language. (Not really, but I am known to spend more time creating systems than actually implementing them.) Since my idea of a date night is achieving security and order through events like calendar planning and goal setting, that's where I first introduced the book to my husband.

Granted, it may not have been the ideal approach to embarking upon a new family strategy, but he humored me and we began to develop our rallying cry—a single sentence we wanted our family to be known for. That rallying cry would also serve as a filter through which we'd make all major decisions as a family.

Once we honed in on what was truly important to us as a nuclear family unit, it became easier to make decisions about the projects, outings, savings goals, and everyday dilemmas that confronted us as a family. Essentially, it helped us move from "good to great" (*Good to Great* by Jim Collins is another book I'd recommend). Instead of settling for what's just "good," we do our best to fill our days only with what's truly great.

The beauty of this exercise is that no two families' mission statements will look the same, in content or in concept. And the most important component of the family mission statement is the communication that goes into creating it together.

As soon as you've created some form of family mission statement that you can all get behind and move forward with together, place it in a high-traffic area of your home so it's continually in sight. Here are just a few ideas for how you can display your newfound family road map:

- Write it on a chalkboard.
- Create a poster.
- Make a fun version on the computer, print it out, and put it in a frame.
- Write it on a mirror with dry-erase markers.
- Clip it to the fridge.
- If nothing else, put it on a Post-it note and stick it to the door you see before going outside so it's a constant reminder before you go anywhere!

Whatever you do, don't forget to let your kids help. Anytime you make your kids part of the process, you automatically make them part of the solution.

Now that we've looked at the emotional component of harmony in the home, let's tackle the physical.

Home Décor That Contributes to Harmony

In my family, our roles are a bit reversed from what tradition would dictate.

My husband is much more skilled when it comes to matters of the home than I am. I'd like to think my prowess lies more in creativity on the computer and in business arenas. That being said, not only am I horrible when it comes to home décor, I also don't believe much of our budget should be lent to it.

In fact, I cringed watching my husband hang pictures in our first home because I was already anticipating repairing the nail holes that would inevitably come when we moved out (even though we had no intention of moving out anytime soon). He humored me by keeping paint colors neutral and buying the majority of our furniture from a second-hand store.

Anytime you make your kids part of the process, you automatically make them part of the solution.

It wasn't long, however, before I noticed a state of unrest in my husband. Upon further digging, I discovered that I was not only thwarting his God-given talent of interior design, but my tendency to be primed for a move at any given moment was robbing our new family of joy.

One of the reasons my husband enjoys decorating so much is the feeling it creates in the hearts of its occupants. He longed for a place to come home to that felt comfortable, welcoming, and most important, recognizable as our unique home, not one of those cookie-cutter model homes builders like to show before a neighborhood is fully developed.

Slowly but surely, he convinced me that home décor can, in fact, lead to harmony. And while it is not the sole component responsible for creating harmony in the home, it is certainly one of them.

In her book *The Nesting Place*, Myquillyn Smith is famous for advising in its subtitle, "It doesn't have to be perfect to be beautiful."[4] In essence, I think that's what my husband was trying to show me all along: that we could create our own version of what a harmonious home looked like by redefining and combining both of our preconceived notions.

It's my belief that where most people make a mistake when it comes to home décor is here: they add before they subtract. People believe they have to buy new stuff to re-create their space, when the key is to declutter first.

In fact, one of the first things a real estate agent will tell you before putting a home on the market is to reduce the number of things occupying space in your home by about 50 percent. You'll be amazed how the simple act of decluttering can make such a profound difference in your home.

When my husband goes in to stage homes before they're put on the market, the first thing he does after decluttering is to analyze what the homeowners already have that can still be used. Sometimes swapping accessories between rooms or rearranging furniture can revitalize the look and feel of your home.

After you repurpose what you can, take the purged items and sell them through either a garage or online sale. If you are on a tiny budget, you can then allocate the money you make toward your new decorating projects. Whatever you don't sell, donate to a local nonprofit that can put them to good use.

Just like with the family mission statement, take time to come together as a family and discuss what you want the culture of your home to look and feel like. Consider allowing each member of the family to choose a special area of the home where they can exert their influence so everyone feels part of the process and the finished product.

Taking the time to create harmony in your home, through the spiritual, emotional, and physical, allows your family to have not only a personal haven but one that will equip you to better go out and make a difference in the world outside your four walls (something we'll be discussing further in section two).

When your home serves you, instead of you being a slave to your home, you also free up time to use your home as a place to welcome others and meet their physical, emotional, and even spiritual needs.

The key component we've focused on from Colossians 3 in this chapter is in verse 14: "Above all, clothe yourselves with love, which binds us all together in perfect harmony" (NLT).

This verse epitomizes the concept of lessons being caught and not taught. As we learned in chapter one, without a foundation of love, nothing worthwhile will ever be accomplished. Yet now we see that as we dig deeper into the power of love, its power is in the harmony it creates, first between us and God and then between our hearts and others.

! Make It Practical

It's one thing to talk about what your family values are; it's quite another to live them out.

The concepts in this chapter can come alive in your home in several ways, but one of my all-time favorites, the tool that has been the most effective with our kids, is a prayer poster.

When I truly came to know the Lord in my midtwenties, I quickly realized I couldn't possibly pray for everyone all the time. So while I knew there would always be spontaneous and continuous prayer in my life, I also knew I needed to get some sort of system going. I wanted to make sure there was consistency in my prayer life, especially surrounding the people and causes I cared about.

So I created categories I would pray for each day, week by week. That didn't mean I couldn't diverge from or add to my prayers, people, and categories, but the categories gave me a nice, simple template to structure my prayers. Which made me think, why couldn't I do something similar for my kiddos?

Since they don't carry a planner or smartphone around yet (thankfully) and are more captivated by pictures than words, I thought a prayer poster would be the best solution. I had also been trying to devise a way for them to remember extended family members we didn't see very often, so this fit the bill perfectly.

Below are the step-by-step directions for our kids prayer poster. You'll want to supervise, but make sure your kids do as much of this as possible so they know it's theirs. (You can also take a look at our kids' prayer poster here at http://samicone.com/kids-prayer-poster/.)

1. Turn a plain sheet of white poster board horizontally.
2. Plot out seven columns evenly spaced across the sheet.
3. Have the kids write a title across the top ("Prayer Poster" will do), skip a space, and write the days of the week at the top of each column.
4. Under the days of the week, write the category of what/who you'll be praying for that day.
5. Find and print pictures to represent those categories or people, so you have a visual reminder of what or who you're praying for. For example, if you decide to pray for our nation every Saturday, you can print, cut out, and then paste a photograph or illustration of the American flag in the Saturday column.

6. Display the prayer poster in a prime area and reference it during your designated family prayer time.

You can come up with your categories any way you see fit, but for a point of reference, here is what and who we pray for each day:

Sunday:	Church (including pastors, missionaries, nonprofit causes we support)
Monday:	Work (jobs, co-workers) and School (teachers, classmates)
Tuesday:	Our Family (our nuclear family)
Wednesday:	Extended Family (on my husband's side)
Thursday:	Extended Family (on my side)
Friday:	Friends (including other couples, kids' friends)
Saturday:	Our Nation (issues surrounding our government and culture)

Whether you're reading this book over months or all in one sitting, you've now reached a point where you've been equipped to set a tone in your home. While our ultimate goal is to raise a generation of world-changers, compassion can never take place outside our homes if we don't first prepare the culture of our homes from which to launch our children.

Here are some other ways to make it practical:

- *Create a family mission statement.* Once you do, display it prominently in your home where every member of your family can not only see it but refer back to it often.
- *Check your calendar.* Determine if your family's giving, spending, and calendar reflect what you value.
- *Redesign your home.* Go through each room of your house and have each family member call out the thing they like most about that space, whether tangible or intangible.

Strive to make everyone's voice heard and represented in some way.

• *Begin decluttering your home.* It's up to you whether you want to include your kids in this activity based on their ages, but I recommend including younger children. Consider tackling a different room or category (such as toys, gear and gadgets, clothes, décor, and even furniture) each week. Once you do, decide whether to sell, donate, or stash the items for a designated period of time to make sure you are really ready to part with them. If you decide to sell the items, especially if they belonged to your kids, consider including your children by holding a garage sale they can help with and then donating the profits to a charity of their choosing.

For more practical tips and guidelines, visit SamiCone.com/UncommonKids.

3

GENTLENESS

Be Careful, Little Ears, What You Hear

Call me an optimist, but I tend to believe I can do anything.

Case in point: I recently developed a minor infatuation with the show *American Ninja Warrior*.

Have you heard of it? It's described as the world's toughest obstacle course; think *Wipeout*, but with fewer jokes and real athletes. It's been a phenomenon in Japan for years but has only recently emerged in the United States.

Being a former tennis pro, I have a tendency to live in the mind of a professional athlete, even though it's been over fifteen years since I've competed in anything that didn't involve a karaoke stage.

Still, as I watched these mountain climbers, weight lifters, and parkour phenoms, I somehow thought I could keep up with them. I'd stand mesmerized in front of the screen while preparing dinner each week, audibly repeating, "I could do that."

While my husband discreetly rolled his eyes, my kids were much quicker to call my bluff.

I determined to prove them wrong.

We'd just witnessed "The Body Prop," where warrior wannabes had to traverse over a pool of water horizontally simply by using their hands and feet to push against two parallel planks.

In an instant (and without much thought, mind you), I planted my hands on our kitchen counter and demanded my husband catch my feet as I kicked them up into the air behind me.

Within seconds of his successfully grabbing my limbs, I unsuccessfully managed to prove my family wrong, falling flat on my face onto our tiled kitchen floor.

I quickly picked myself up, dusted myself off, and confessed, "Maybe it is a little harder than it looks on television."

Thankfully, my kids made sure I was okay before they busted out laughing. But now anytime I even begin to utter, "I could do that" while watching *American Ninja Warrior*, my kids just smile and say, "Sure, Mom."

Perception Is Everything

What can we learn from this little episode (other than the fact that I have to actually do some training before I apply for the next season of *American Ninja Warrior*)?

Our kids are much more perceptive than we often give them credit for.

In fact, one of the most common mistakes we make as parents is assuming our kids don't hear us. I would argue that they do in fact hear most of what we have to say; whether they choose to listen is a completely different story.

Just think about it. How many times has this happened? Your kids are watching a movie while you're talking to a friend on the phone about a topic not necessarily for little ears. Their glazed-over expression communicates they're completely entranced, yet once you hang up the phone, your oldest immediately asks what you meant when you said, "_____."

Because our children don't heed every word we throw their way, we mistakenly believe they don't hear *any* of what we say the first time we say it. This misbelief carefully adds up to countless careless conversations around our children.

Our kids are much more perceptive than we often give them credit for.

And the carelessness doesn't stop there.

This lazy attitude can pervade our routine. We don't want our own desires and schedules altered, so we allow our children to watch more of what we watch, listen to more of what we listen to, and participate in more of what we participate in.

Now, this would be fine if we refrained from much screen time, only listened to Christian CDs, and lived in a protective bubble. And we all know that even in Christian circles, we are all imperfect people who do and say imperfect things, so even then our kids aren't completely "safe."

TV Time

Let's go back to the example of something trivial like television.

I'll be the first to admit that because I grew up as a latchkey kid, I have an unnatural attachment to the television. While I never sit blindly and watch television without also doing another activity, I do enjoy having it on as background noise.

So it should come as no surprise that we've never banned television from our home, but we have tried to keep clear rules about our kids' television consumption: only certain channels and only during certain times of the day.

As our children have entered the elementary years and now occasionally have time to watch a show with us before bed (like a cooking competition or the aforementioned *American Ninja Warrior*), we've had to put even stricter rules in place because of the commercials during prime-time television hours.

But I should warn you, don't allow your kids to watch reruns of your favorite '90s prime-time comedies unless you're ready to answer questions like, "What was that word that rhymed with witch?"

And it should go without saying that you need to have a speech prepared about the colloquialism commonly used these days that refers to that barnyard animal found in the stable when Jesus was born.

Much like our kids will learn how to eat healthfully if we do, or put away their clothes if we do, our kids speak what they hear from us—or what we allow them to hear.

Gentleness

The next key component in raising uncommon kids is gentleness, and it is best found and modeled in the parent-child relationship.

MENTOR MOMENT
HOW TO TALK TO YOUR KIDS

From the moment I met Diana Sumpter at church, I knew I was going to love her. Her quick-witted, fast-talking personality and heart for others immediately drew me in. But we also shared the same story in how our tendency to react had made a negative impact on our daughters. Here is the moment that changed her forever:

> I can remember it was at the end of June (which for an Independent Mary Kay consultant is one of our biggest months). I was talking on the phone when my daughter, Samantha, who was about four at the time, came up to me and wanted to ask me something. I put

Colossians 3:19 and 21 remind us: "Husbands, love your wives and never treat them harshly. . . . Fathers, do not aggravate your children, or they will become discouraged" (NLT).

The Bible provides clear directives for not just what we should say but how we should say it, and gentleness clearly starts with us.

On more than one occasion—in fact on a weekly basis—I tell my husband that what he says to me may be correct, but how he sometimes says it makes me tune him out. As humans, our defense mechanism is quick to emerge whenever we feel we are being attacked, whether physically or verbally.

Even if we speak in a slightly louder tone than normal, our sheer size and presence looming over our children can cause fear and shock in them. While a reverential fear is healthy (and even desirable in the form of respect toward God and parents), scare tactics are not what we want to resort to when parenting.

The *Evangelical Dictionary of Biblical Theology* defines gentleness as "sensitivity of disposition and kindness of behavior, founded on strength and prompted by love."[1] We also see in Proverbs 15:1 and 25:15 that gentle words wield great power, not to

my hand over the mouthpiece on the phone, looked at her sternly, and barked, "What do you want?" I was very rude.

She got huge crocodile tears and said, "Mommy, why won't you talk to me like you talk to your Mary Kay ladies?"

And so I told the woman on the phone I had to go, hung up, and from that point forward, I made a commitment to talk to my daughter through the same filter as the people I worked with. It totally changed our relationship to create a safe place for her to come to me about anything.[2]

Diana Sumpter is a wife, mom of one, grandmother of one, military veteran, and Mary Kay National Sales Director.

mention that Job's counsels were well received because he spoke them gently (Job 29:22).

Gentleness is often mistaken for meekness, but I'd argue that it takes someone with real strength to show grace and gentleness, especially when they have the authority (or perceived authority) to exercise their might and muscle.

Even if you're like me and have a tendency to "share the truth" more often than perhaps you need to, this still needs to be done gently, as evidenced in 1 Peter 3:15: "In your hearts revere Christ as Lord. Always be prepared to give an answer to everyone who asks you to give the reason for the hope that you have. But do this with gentleness and respect."

Intentionally Invest

One of the worst ways we discredit our children is not just by speaking ill to them but by speaking ill of them. As parents, we are quick to label our children—for good or bad. These labels become part of our vernacular and pop out easily when chatting with friends, such as referring to individual kids as "my easy one" or "the funny one"—or worse yet, "my difficult one."

> *One of the worst ways we discredit our children is not just by speaking ill to them but by speaking ill of them.*

Not only will your children begin to adopt these labels if they hear them repeatedly, but they tend to take on the opposite label if they realize a certain attribute is already taken. For instance, if one child constantly hears you calling a sibling "the smart one," they assume that role is filled in the family and set out to discover a new way they can stand out. As you can imagine, that doesn't always emerge in a positive way.

Instead, intentionally invest an equal amount of time to speaking well of your children, both in public and private.

Nothing does more for a child's heart than for them to "overhear" you praising them publicly. Likewise, make it a practice to greet them first thing in the morning with a positive word and send them to bed at night with another positive trait about themselves to meditate on as they go to sleep.

Just as you are charged to help your children discern God's voice, you also want them to hear your voice speaking blessings over them in the quiet places of their minds and hearts.

There is power in *our* words, but the Word also confirms the power of even just one word. After all, theologian John Piper reminds us of this very fact in his book *The Power of Words and the Wonder of God*:

> Words carry immeasurable significance: The universe was created with a word; Jesus healed and cast out demons with a word; rulers have risen and fallen by their words; Christians have worshiped through words of song, confession, and preaching. Even in our technological age, politics, education, business, and relationships center on words.
>
> Since the tongue is such a powerful force—for good or evil—we are wise to ask: What would homes, churches, schools, even the public square be like if we used words with Christian intentionality and eloquence?[3]

Parenting Mirror: Be the Change

Someone wise once wrote, "You must be the change you want to see in the world." And it's true. Before we can ever hope to change our kids, we must first become agents of change and model that behavior ourselves.

As parents, we must model grace and gentleness in our own words before we can ever expect our kids to emulate those qualities.

In a world where more and more is becoming acceptable and less is considered vulgar, we must institute a new standard for ourselves.

Below are several simple ways you can begin to set a new tone in your household that will define communication, not only for your family but for how your children communicate with others.

1. The Power of Positive

As we saw in our Mentor Moment, the power of positive words trickles down. It's been said that it takes ten positive compliments to make up for one negative comment that's made to someone. I've never been able to shake the powerful image I first read about in the book *The Ultimate Gift* by Jim Stovall.[4]

It's a tale about a boy whose grandfather required him to hammer a nail in their fence every time he uttered something negative. After some time had passed, he allowed him to remove a nail from the fence each time he said something positive. The boy soon discovered that he'd trained his speech to where he spoke more positive than negative words, yet nothing could be done to fill the holes left by the nails.

The point was this: even when the nails were removed—representing the replacement of negative with positive—the marks and scars remained. Even if we apologize after letting negative remarks fly from our mouths, we cannot erase the original effects of those words on the receiver. The sooner we train ourselves to respond in a positive way, even when angry, the sooner the trickle effect will take place in our homes.

2. The Power of Pause

Some of us think to speak, while others speak to think; usually each type marries the other. This is certainly true in our home.

While my husband likes to take time alone to process incidents before he speaks about them, I allow my thoughts to form as the words barrel out of my mouth. Neither is right or wrong; they're merely different.

When it comes to dealing with others, however, especially our kids, we've found it helpful to take a moment to pause before saying anything we could potentially regret. In the heat of the moment, it becomes easy to hurl out insults and hurtful remarks in an effort to match the pain we experience. Instead, we've instituted a three-count rule: before saying anything, we ask our kids to count to three.

This power of pause not only allows for some breathing room in typically tense situations, but it makes each of us consider whether what we are about to say is something we actually want to say.

3. The Power of Perspective

We are all limited by our unique experiences and perspectives. The opposite of gentleness is wrath, which usually emerges when we believe our rights are being violated.

The truth is that we won't always agree on the same perspective, even if everyone in the family experiences the same event at the same time. We have to be willing to concede that our way is not necessarily the right way. Our willingness to approach a situation from a new perspective could not only broaden our own knowledge base but also soften the hearts of those whose perspective we're taking.

In the next chapter, I'll go into further detail about sibling relationships, but it begs to be brought up here. The one thing that irks me the most is the tone my children frequently use when speaking to each other. It's not uncommon for me to hear snarky, sassy, or sarcastic comments casually being batted back and forth between them. Yet before I can criticize or correct them, I need to realize where they most likely learned that behavior in the first place. The real culprit and teacher is how we interact with them day in and day out.

Now, please hear me. I'm not saying to be passive, never raise your voice, and let your kids get away with murder. What I am saying is follow the guidelines above and, as much as humanly possible, be intentional with not only what is coming out of your mouth but also how and when it's being presented.

Timing Is Everything

One early parenting technique we learned was to give a five-minute warning before moving on to another task or leaving somewhere. We were told kids find security in knowing what is to come and don't like to be caught off guard.

We've found the validity of this tip especially true when it comes to talking with our kids. For example, expecting our kids to comprehend and act on our commands while they're watching television is futile, just as is trying to discipline them in a store or in front of their friends. While it's important to deal with disobedience in the moment, sometimes the best action is telling them you're going to deal with it later (and then actually following through!). Showing your kids respect helps model exactly what it is you expect to receive from them.

Case in point: I'm not much of a yeller, but I've also been known to lose my patience in public. It didn't take me long to realize public shaming doesn't go far in getting desired results from my children. Instead, I've found an ace in the hole, so to speak: my ability to speak French.

While my kids are far from fluent, I started teaching them both French and sign language from the time they were about six months old. Not only did this dispel most of the "terrible twos" because they were able to communicate with us using sign language, but their knowing some French allows me to give them commands, and even more stern directives, in public without embarrassing them.

How, you ask?

Everything sounds better in a foreign language, doesn't it? While that's not entirely true, most onlookers have no idea what I'm saying to my kids, keeping them from public humiliation while I'm still able to get my point across without yelling in public. For our family, it's a win/win.

While you may not speak another language, consider other ways you can model gentleness in your parent-child relationship: a nonverbal cue, a designated area you both go to resolve conflict, or even a once-a-week check-in to ask your child's perspective on what's going well in your relationship as well as what could use some improvement.

Before anyone can expect to change the world, they must start with changing themselves and influencing those closest to them.

After all, our goal in raising uncommon kids is not to create robots that love others on command and obey our every whim. Even God doesn't treat us that way. Rather, it's important to cultivate this tone of gentleness and respect under your own roof so your children are equipped to replicate it outside your home.

When you begin to implement this brand of intentional gentleness, your family will soon reap the rewards in other relationships as well.

❗Make It Practical

Before anyone can expect to change the world, they must start with changing themselves and influencing those closest to them. Matthew 12:34–35 reminds us that "the mouth speaks what the heart is full of." If we expect our children to pour out love to others, their hearts must first be filled with the love, joy, gentleness, and tolerance that can only be learned from and modeled by us as

we have learned from and sought to model our heavenly Father.
Here are a few ideas to help drive this point home:

- *Parents switch roles with kids for a day*: Want to help your
  kids experience what it's really like to be you? Switch roles
  with them for a day. While children are typically thrilled
  at the prospect of ordering around their parents, the tides
  typically turn once they discover the new balance of work
  and play. Even if you don't do this for an entire day, make
  sure to save time to celebrate the switching back of roles and
  debrief what everyone experienced.

- *One-on-one parent-child date*: Even though you may already
  feel like you spend all day with your kids, nothing can re-
  place intentional one-on-one time in an activity of the child's
  choosing. I've written about this in more detail here: http://
  samicone.com/make-time-for-kid-dates/.

- *Lunch box notes*: Whether you print out something from
  Pinterest or write "I love you" on a napkin with a Sharpie,
  take an extra moment to add some thoughtfulness to your
  child's lunch box. If they're older or don't take a lunch to
  school, consider dropping an encouragement into their backpacks or even texting a quick note of love and encouragement
  during the day.

- *Speak positive*: Purpose as a family to speak only positive
  words for an entire day. That means no complaining, name-
  calling, or negative comments for a twenty-four-hour period.
  And don't forget to come up with a creative consequence for
  anyone who flubs, such as putting a dollar in a jar. At the
  end of the day that money can be donated to church or to a
  cause of your children's choosing.

- *Day of yes*: For a predetermined amount of time, agree to
  say yes to whatever your kids ask (as long as it doesn't involve
  money or inflicting harm).

- *Let your children deal with their mistakes:* Don't be so quick to clean up all your children's messes for them. Think about it. It's better to help your kids process their flubs while they're living with you in their school years than to raise them in a bubble and then send them off to college without a hint of what the world will throw at them.

For more practical tips and guidelines, visit SamiCone.com/UncommonKids.

4

BEARING WITH

The Secret of Sibling Love

Thirty-one-year-old Tracy Barnes had earned a spot on the 2014 U.S. Olympic biathlon team, yet she declined it to allow the woman next in line to go to Sochi.

That woman was her twin sister, Lanny Barnes.

Lanny had fallen ill over the qualifying weekend, missing three of the final four selection races in Italy, and her hopes of going to a third Olympics had vanished. Only five U.S. women go to the Olympics for this event, and Lanny was just out of the running until Tracy informed her of a decision she had made before that final race.

"Love is selfless dedication," Tracy said, according to an article on 3WireSports.com. "Love means giving up your dream so someone else can realize theirs."[1]

While most of us will never come close to going to the Olympics, we can help our kids embrace the spirit of sibling love modeled by these Olympian sisters.

But how do we coach our kids so they will have achieved this kind of love and appreciation for each other by the time they're out from under our roof?

While there may not be an easy answer, the Bible does offer a clear answer: "Bear with each other" (Col. 3:13).

Sibling Love

If I could write a book solely on how to successfully get siblings to love each other better, I would be rich.

Crazy, but rich.

Alas, I'm afraid none of us as parents will ever uncover that exact secret or science. In fact, I'm not sure if there is any more common conversation or Facebook post from moms of elementary school–aged kids than, "Please tell me I'm not the only one trying to keep my kids from killing each other right now."

After all, how is it that these perfect babies, who enter the world with smiles and sweetness, just years later seem hell-bent on bringing down the person they share a room with?

As an only child, I of all people have a difficult time understanding sibling love. And the concept of loving multiple children with "all your heart" seemed contradictory on some level.

So how then do we expect children to understand this concept?

If you have more than one child, I don't have to tell you about the dichotomy of sibling love.

After you have your first baby, whether by birth or adoption, it seems nearly impossible to reconcile that you could ever love another child as much as you love your first. And yet once that second child is put into your arms, it's like an entirely new piece of your heart that wasn't there before opens up, not taking anything away from the first child, but expanding to fully love this new creation.

Just as you love each of your children differently, you need to coach your children how to love each other differently.

Unique Love

Seeing as we cannot parent each of our kids the same way, we cannot expect them to love each other the same way. While this notion is fairly common among adults, we rarely apply it to young siblings.

Why, you ask?

For starters, it takes time, a luxury many of us do not have when raising young children. Not only do we have to take the time to individually discern how each child receives love best, but then we have to spend an equal if not greater amount of time conditioning their siblings to love them in that way.

I find Gary Chapman and Ross Campbell describe it best in their book *The 5 Love Languages of Children*.[2] In essence, they lay out five different ways we all receive love, but propose that each of us has a primary and secondary love language. If you don't "speak" someone's love language to them, even if you're doing something to show them love, they will not receive it as such.

For example, let's say I spend a full day with one of my children, taking them shopping and spending quality time, yet never having any meaningful conversation. If my child's love language is words of affirmation, then that time would be (for the sake of this exercise) essentially worthless.

On the other hand, if I had taken ten minutes after school to sit across from that same child in our kitchen, ask them about their day, give them my undivided attention, and then point out things I've heard or observed about them that I admire and share how proud I am of them, their love tank will overflow!

It seems so basic, and yet I've found it to be so true in my family. Let me paint a picture for how this works with each of my own two children.

My firstborn, Kariss Nevaeh, is a typical firstborn child: driven, dependable, independent, task-oriented, and yes, even legalistic when it comes to following rules and maintaining fairness. However, she is also an artistic little girl who loves animals and is currently obsessed with Hawaii and all things having to do with the islands. As much as I (and her little brother) would like her to be, she is not a cuddler and has a hard time abandoning the rational in life.

I've also recently come to realize that she has an almost crippling perfectionist tendency that prevents her from wanting to join any group lessons/activities. The fear of "not doing it right" prevents her from enjoying learning something new in a group setting. What I first assumed to be laziness turned out to be a self-preservation technique.

Once I realized these things about her, I could stop trying to force a square peg into a round hole. I called upon friends of mine and even past teachers she'd clicked with. These folks possessed different strengths than me and could help Kariss learn more about topics where I wasn't equipped to guide her. And I also was finally able to explain to her younger brother that her cold reception every time he tried to smother her didn't mean she didn't love him, but reflected a nonverbal cry to love her differently.

Which brings me to my second born, Britton Jerick.

Sometimes I wonder if he was born a lap dog. To say physical touch is his love language is an understatement; if he could sit on me all day he would. But don't mistake that for being shy; he's the life of the party. This kid cracks us up constantly. It's hard not to smile when looking at his crazy hair and the top part of his cheeks that puff up when he's laughing.

In fact, I'll be the first to admit it: we underestimated his abilities for a long time because we focused on his cuteness. If I had to confess any character flaw, it would be that he's learned to leverage that cute factor to manipulate life to work in his favor at home and at school. But since he's been in school, we've been able to see abilities we didn't before, like a knack for math and a natural ability in sports like gymnastics and tennis.

Just as we've had to coach Britton not to jump on his sister with hugs and kisses every chance he gets, we've also had to encourage Kariss to reach out to him with a milder form of the physical affection he so desperately craves.

Please hear me clearly: recognizing another's unique love style does not provide a free pass to ignore every other love language.

Because all of us most often give love in the way we like to receive it, loving outside our "borders" can be challenging. However, it's up to us as parents to help our children recognize how their siblings best receive love and then provide tangible examples for how they can live out that sibling love.

The Secret of Sibling Love

So why can getting our kids to love each other be so hard?

Are we doomed to years of merely keeping our kids from killing each other, praying that one day they will eventually have a close relationship in their young adulthood?

They always seem to start out cute, right? I mean, I know I've got a picture somewhere of my children hugging each other nearly to the point of strangulation.

So what exactly happens between years two and eighteen that causes such a great divide in our kids? And even more important, how do we overcome it?

I would daresay the secret of sibling love is this: it depends on the sibling.

A friend recently blogged about how she noticed her son was not treating his little sister the way he should. When she and her husband pulled him aside, he broke down, crying over the fact that he wasn't acting the way God would want him to and confessing, "It's just so hard sometimes!"

Don't we all have moments when we want to cry out in that same way?

Deep within their hearts is the cry not only to be loved, but to love in return.

I loved hearing about the honest heart's cry from this little boy because it reminded me what I believe to be true of all our children: deep within their hearts is the cry not only to be loved, but to love in return. There is, however, so much at war around them, pulling them from doing what our Creator designed them to do.

So what do we do as parents?

We model love.

Just as we love our kids equally, yet uniquely, we need to mentor them on how to do the same with each other. We help them to find one thing they love about their sibling to focus on (like I recounted Ms. Donna instructing me in chapter 1), and then we coach them how to love through the rest.

Surprisingly Good

Before we throw our hands into the air and assume all children are completely clueless in this plight to show compassion to their siblings, an example from my family's recent Disney World trip may shed some light on what's really going on deep within our children's hearts.

My aunt and uncle gave our kids a gift card to use specifically during the vacation. We revealed the gift card situation on day one, informing them they each had fifty dollars to use however they wished. We hoped it would make them responsible and not ask for a souvenir in every shop because they knew they only had a certain amount of their own money to spend. We also wanted them to be grateful for the gift they received.

Instead, we ended up holding it over their heads as a reward for good behavior. Pretty soon our attention was completely off the vacation and consumed with keeping a scorecard for who had how much money left and who was allowed to spend it or not. We were trying to shove gratitude down their throats, using consumerism as a vehicle to do it.

After yet another reprimand on how they needed to start being grateful for where we were and start treating each other better, my eight-year-old son approached me with a saddened look and said, "Mom, I need to ask you a question."

With very concerned eyes, he asked, "Do you think you can help me come up with a way to not react so negatively to Kariss when she bugs me?"

In that moment, I was so struck with his kindness and wisdom. And I told him so.

I looked at him earnestly and affirmed him for what a mature question that was. I wanted to honor his thoughtfulness by taking some time to think about an equally thoughtful response to help him.

As parents, it's hard to remember that our kids aren't intentionally trying to drive us nuts. I think it's safe to say that no matter how old we are, all of us strive to please our parents; the problem arises when we lack the tools to do so.

Sometimes it is a literal lack of understanding; other times it is a lack of patience. Whatever the case, it is our responsibility to help our children understand and to equip them with the proper tools.

It took me a full day to come up with a response for my son. First, I thought about how one of our kids' biggest triggers is when they point at or poke each other. There's just something about a pointed finger that antagonizes them. Second, we've sometimes asked them to stop and think about how they would feel if something tragic happened to the other. Oftentimes pushing away the heat of the moment to look at the bigger picture has helped them regain perspective.

So based on those thoughts, when my son returned to me with the question on the plane ride home, I had one idea.

I suggested that when his sister was really bugging him, he put a flat hand on her shoulder or on her leg in a comforting way. This flat hand should serve as a reminder to stop and breathe before he speaks, but also by touching her, hopefully he will remember the blessing of having his sister physically there with him and be reminded of what life might be like if she were ever taken away from him.

Honestly, I don't know if it will work or if it will stick, but my son communicated something very important to me with that question.

For starters, he desperately wanted to love his sister well and be sweet at the same time, but he lacked the skills to do it consistently.

MENTOR MOMENT
FACE-TO-FACE

One of my mentors, Catherine Hickem, told me this story about her children:

My son and daughter, just fourteen months apart, had been arguing one weekend. Sibling relationships are the longest relationships we can have and I wanted them to have the skills to resolve their differences in a healthy manner. Like most parents, I also did not want to spend my life acting as a referee with them.

My mind immediately went to the old pew we had sitting in the front room of our house. Instead of spending my time trying to come up with a mutually beneficial solution to the situation at hand, I challenged my children with that exact task.

I instructed them to sit next to each other on that church pew, face-to-face. I put twenty minutes on a timer and told them they

He told me he needed something tangible to help him when his human nature overtakes his spirit.

Think about it. Don't we all have similar struggles? What do we do as adults when we face struggles? We have accountability partners. We have Bible verses memorized. We even have apps that help us. But we have to fill the gap for our children who know in their heads what is right yet cannot do it in their own strength.

I loved hearing that story because it reminded me that even with all the parenting theories swirling around out there today, it's not always up to us to figure things out for our children; sometimes we just need to provide them the opportunity to work it out themselves.

Our family even watched this play out on television when *Duck Dynasty* brothers Willie and Jase Robertson got caught bickering by their mom and she made them "hug it out." It just goes to show that you're never too old to go back to the basics.

Beneath all of the bickering is a cry to be loved, and it's up to us as parents to model for our children how to love in return. If we

needed to arrive at a win-win solution. Failure to do so would mean they would spend the rest of the day in their rooms, alone.

Fortunately for all of us, they resolved their differences and both children seemed proud of their accomplishment. This protocol became their new method of problem-solving and taught them skills they would later use in other relationships.

Sure, the results could have been devastating to the entire family, but I've found it pays to stand your ground on the big mountains if you want to be able to not only tolerate but enjoy the smaller hills of life and parenting. After a scenario and consequence like this, they rarely made that same mistake again![3]

Catherine Hickem is the author of *Regret Free Parenting* and *Heaven in Her Arms* as well as a psychotherapist, executive coach, women's ministry leader, and founder of Dash Organization.

fail to recognize that passionate need and act to meet it, we may be missing a golden opportunity to show our children how to love.

Lost in Expression

While our kids may truly love each other deep down, the sentiment can get lost in the expression. Couple that with the way we believe our children should behave and you often end up with a confusing combination of emotions.

Rather than meddling, I've decided to stand back and watch when my kids genuinely demonstrate love to each other. After all, someday when our kids have no one but each other from their family of origin to lean on, those are the moments they'll remember, not the ones when we coaxed them into our own definition of love.

While there may not be one simple secret to getting your kids to love each other, you may be surprised to find the key already lies in their own hearts.

The Bible tells us to "be completely humble and gentle; be patient, bearing with one another in love" (Eph. 4:2). Sometimes that's easier said than done.

So what do we do as parents?

Love.

It's what makes the world go 'round, right? But what about when we aren't "feeling it"? Or worse, what if we love deeply but get hurt in the process? Perhaps we've reached the point where we don't feel very loving anymore.

What then?

Loving When You Don't Feel Like It

I can tell you from firsthand experience; I've been there.

How is it possible that in one simple moment, everything you once thought you knew about love can be carelessly ripped away from you? And yet it happens. (Probably more often than we would like to admit.)

So what do we do when (not if) "it" happens?

When tragedy knocks on our door.

When doubt creeps in.

When we feel we've done all we can.

When we just become too tired to keep on keeping on.

We love.

But not in a greeting-card sort of way. We love in a Jesus-dying-on-the-cross kind of way.

God never promised love would be easy. He never promised love would be consistent, without ebbs and flows. And he certainly never promised that we'd figure it out this side of heaven.

Can I get an "Amen"?

What God did promise is:

- He loved us first (1 John 4:19).
- He will love us with an everlasting love (Jer. 31:3).
- He will never give us more than we can bear (1 Cor. 10:13).

And though we may never fully comprehend the how, why, or what of the word *love*, we can rest assured that nothing we are facing is outside of the reach of our almighty, all-knowing, all-seeing heavenly Father.

When we don't know, we trust.

When we don't feel, we pray.

And when we grieve, we go to the feet of the One who paid the ultimate sacrifice for our sins.

I'll confess it's not easy. But when you find yourself asking God how you can possibly love the unlovable, he'll tell you to focus more on him and less on whoever or whatever it is you feel can't be loved.

The same holds true when modeling love for our children.

Modeling Love

Modeling is different from teaching. Children observe and learn from how you operate within boundaries in your own world. They watch how you treat them, your spouse, and your work. And they emulate you, for good or bad.

While you may already believe the truths we've discussed here, convincing your children of the same can be challenging. Too often, they focus on the action that has hurt them rather than the person and circumstances behind the actual event.

Love is not simply a feeling; it's an action.

Helping them see the root cause of why we do what we do will not only help little ones better understand how to love others but will ultimately help them take responsibility for their own actions and feelings.

While none of us is perfect, we serve a God who is, and we were made in his image (Gen. 1:27).

So for those of you who don't feel loved, have lost your will to love, or are at your wit's end trying to model love for your children, I encourage you to go back to the Source of all love. Love is not simply a feeling; it's an action. Even when we don't *feel* loving, we can *choose* to exhibit the love that comes from our heavenly Father.

Before we can move confidently to demonstrating compassion in our neighborhood, we must first cement the truth of Colossians 3:13 to "bear with each other." Modeling compassion in our homes is absolutely essential if we ever hope for our children to understand what it truly means to have a compassionate heart toward others.

! Make It Practical

For siblings (or any children for that matter) to truly understand what it means to "bear with each other" as laid out in Colossians 3:13, practical application must be put into place.

Start with coaching your kids to focus on love instead of justice. From there, encourage them to iterate at least one good thing about each of the close relationships in their lives, especially their sibling(s). Finally, challenge them to find at least one good thing in every situation, even the bad ones they discover themselves in the midst of.

Perhaps my favorite tip for helping kids to discover the power of their words and actions toward each other is by using Speak Love Penny Jars. (This is just one of my tips from this list: http://samicone.com/how-to-keep-your-kids-honest-30-ways-30-days/.)

Speak Love Penny Jar instructions:

- Get one clear jar (mason jars without tops work great for this) for each child and label each one with that child's name.

- Fill each jar with the same number of pennies as there are days in the month.

- Every time one of your children does something good, kind, or unexpected, add a penny to their jar.

- Every time a child does something mean, says something unkind, or is disrespectful, subtract a penny from their jar.

- Anytime one of your children is mean or disrespectful to one of their siblings, take a penny from their jar and place it in their sibling's jar.

- At the end of the month, count how many pennies each child has compared to how many they started with. Be careful not to let your kids play the comparison game with each other, but rather focus their attention on the individual progress they made. You can either let them keep the "profit" or roll it over to the next month, should you decide to keep the penny jars going.

- Of course, for older children you can do the same thing with nickels, dimes, quarters, or even dollars. The important thing is to use a clear jar so everyone in the family can easily keep track of their own progress throughout the month.

More ways to make it practical:

- *Encourage your kids to do one of their sibling's chores one day.* Explain how a simple act of kindness can break the battle cycle siblings often find themselves in.
- *Focus on love, not justice.* Life isn't always fair, and the sooner our kids grasp that concept, the better. I often think about the peanut butter commercial where there's only enough bread left for one sandwich to share between two siblings. The mom gives the older child permission to cut the sandwich, and the boy of course makes one half bigger than the other. But then she gives the younger son the choice of which half to keep for himself. While the younger son still chose the bigger half for himself in the end, the choice got the kids to stop and think, perhaps spurring a different outcome next time. Try a simple exercise like this with your kids to reinforce the idea of putting their siblings before themselves.
- *Find at least one good thing in every situation.* We're quick to praise God in the good, but often equally quick to question him in the darker days. Whether you find your family stuck in traffic or in the midst of a sickness that's swept over the entire household, start a practice of finding something positive in every circumstance and thanking God that his plans are always better than our own (Isa. 55).

For more practical tips and guidelines, visit SamiCone.com/UncommonKids.

YOUR ATTITUDE TOWARD OTHERS

Now that we recognize the foundation for raising uncommon kids starts at home (and more important, in our own hearts as parents), we can begin to look at how this manifests itself on the other side of our front doors.

But never forget, our homes exist even outside their four walls.

You see, if we're going to teach our kids to be compassionate, they must first become considerate. Common kids think first about how life will benefit them and then may eventually think about how to help others.

Uncommon kids, on the other hand, learn to look at the world through others' eyes and then consider the impact it plays on their own life.

By definition, to be considerate means considering how others will feel. It's a "you go first" mentality. If we all lived by this rule, the only arguments we'd be having would literally be who gets to go last.

Instead, our kids jockey for the best seat, the biggest gift, and the most prestigious accolades.

In her podcast *Enjoying Everyday Life*, Bible teacher Joyce Meyer says, "We're called to love others and control ourselves, when really we're more often concerned with loving ourselves and controlling others."[1]

It's one thing to teach our kids to be obedient to us as parents and civil with their siblings, but it's another thing entirely to instill a sense of consideration and compassion that applies to their close relationships outside of the nucleus of our immediate family.

If we're going to teach our kids to be compassionate, they must first become considerate.

Hopefully, by this juncture you're beginning to see that raising uncommon kids is much more than drilling in automated responses kids know to spit out when they're in our presence, only to have them act out whenever we're not watching. If we want our kids to go against the grain and be able to stand on their own two feet even when apart from us, they need to grasp the characteristics of forgiveness, wisdom, patience, and kindness.

In this section, we'll look at how to take the principles we learned in the first four chapters in partnership with forgiveness, wisdom, patience, and kindness and apply them to our relationships with our extended family, school friends, church group, and neighborhood.

5

FORGIVENESS

Respect What Your Kids Need to Know

Have you ever sat down for a "heart to heart" with your kids and then walked away feeling like they didn't take away anything from your "brilliant" speech?

As a mom, I'm guilty of imposing my jaded adult brain on my child's forgiving mind one too many times. I feel as though I have to share every bit of wisdom and knowledge I possess every opportunity I have to speak to them. The truth of the matter is that studies have shown they only tune into us for about twenty seconds at a time.

Let's be honest: our kids don't need to hear about every detail of every experience we've ever gone through. They're kids, after all.

But how can we be sure our children aren't ignoring the good we demonstrate and only picking up on the bad?

Forgiveness or Bitterness?

The concept of forgiveness isn't always the easiest for kids to grasp, but sometimes life deals us circumstances that force us to choose between forgiveness and bitterness.

During a very rough spot in our marriage, I became concerned that our kids might know too little about what was going on but may have experienced too much.

I felt compelled to sit them down for a talk, but wasn't sure exactly how, where, or when to pull it off. After all, I didn't want to scare them about what was happening if they were totally oblivious, but at the same time, I felt they needed to be treated with respect and were owed some answers to certain questions, if they had them.

So one night after our Celebrate Recovery Step Study[1] group, my husband and I asked our kids if they knew why we were going to "Sunday night church."

Without too much concern, our daughter responded, "So you can be a better mommy and daddy."

Honestly, I think that may have been what we told her when we'd started our road to marital rehabilitation, and we affirmed her accuracy, but went on to tell her there was more to it.

"You know how you love your brother, but you don't always like him? And sometimes you hurt each other's feelings, even though you don't mean to? Well, Mommy and Daddy have each made some mistakes and have hurt each other in different ways. So we've been going to meet with other people who can help us talk through our feelings, pray with us, and point us in a healthier direction so we can communicate and love each other better, because we don't ever want to get divorced."

Kariss interrupted, "You're getting a *divorce*?!" (Again, it's amazing how that's what she heard out of all my other comments.)

I reassured her, "No, we *don't* want to get a divorce. That's why we're working hard to change how we do things so we can be better together."

She sat back in her seat, feeling better for the moment, and so I took this opportunity to ask an even riskier question of our children. "Do you have any memories of Mommy and Daddy fighting?"

While we'd done our best amid our own strife to shield our children from any unpleasantries, I wasn't ignorant to the fact that children are amazingly perceptive and can still read through our facades.

Britton, it seemed, had stayed blissfully unaware through it all, but my heart stopped when Kariss admitted, "I do remember you arguing once."

Once? That's it? I was honestly stunned and pressed a bit harder.

"Do you remember when that was or what was going on when we were arguing?"

She thought for a second and said, "I can't remember exactly; it was back when we were living in our apartment."

That had been over a year and a half earlier!

Despite dealing with the unthinkable as a married couple over the eight months prior (a circumstance that included a time of marital separation), our children had no specific recollection of us in strife.

Were we deceiving our children? Far from it. We communicated we were in a period of change. We shared about the purpose of a counselor. We even discussed the need to change our schedule for a defined period of time.

What we did not do was scare, threaten, or shame our children. We did not leave them completely in the dark, nor did we share too much.

Failing to Forgive

For our kids to cultivate a character of forgiveness, they need to understand that none of us is above failure, but it's how we move forward after failure that matters.

Romans 3:23 expands on this, saying we are all sinners saved by grace.

Romans 6:1 goes on to say, "What shall we say, then? Shall we go on sinning so that grace may increase?"

On the contrary. Because we have received such an extravagant gift, we ought to conduct ourselves in a way that not only shows gratitude but also demonstrates ultimate respect for the Giver of that gift.

In his book *Failing Forward*, John Maxwell speaks specifically to the importance of what you choose to do after the failure itself:

> In life, the question is not if you will have problems, but how you are going to deal with your problems. . . . The first important step in weathering failure is learning not to personalize it. . . . The essence of man is imperfection. Know that you're going to make mistakes. . . . God uses people who fail—'cause there aren't any other kind around. If you know who you are, make the changes you must in order to learn and grow, and then give everything you've got to your dreams, you can achieve anything your heart desires. Past hurts can make you bitter or better—it's up to you. Start by acknowledging the pain. Forgive others or yourself if need be.[2]

Too often, we fail and then fall down the slippery slope of unforgiveness, not toward others but toward ourselves. We trap ourselves in a cage bound by chains of bitterness, hurt, and resentment.

Sure, we may say we're fighting for justice or holding ourselves to a higher standard, but when we fail to forgive ourselves or those around us, all we're doing is imposing our own beliefs upon others.

Too often, we fail and then fall down the slippery slope of unforgiveness, not toward others but toward ourselves.

We've witnessed the devastating effects such thinking can have.

Just look at the increase in school violence in recent years. What previously existed as an unfortunate, occasional occurrence has now become commonplace in the news to the point where parents purchase bulletproof backpacks for their preteens.

What turns these adolescents into murderers? While we will never know the true depths of a killer's mind, one factor consistently discussed is a lack of feeling valued by their family and wanting to "get back" at them.

Paralysis of Unforgiveness

While many of us will never allow our minds to fall into such depths of darkness, most of us can relate to the pain and paralysis of unforgiveness, especially when it relates to our family of origin.

Once we marry, we're called to "leave and cleave" according to Genesis—in essence, to become of one body and mind with our spouse and create a new family. But that does not mean our own upbringing will not play a factor in how that new family will take shape. On the contrary, it has everything to do with how your future family could look.

The family each of us grows up in shapes us and serves as the school in which we learn to be who we are. While we may not always agree with what or how our family taught us, it's where major core beliefs begin to take root, including everything from our sense of self to how we deal with others and get our needs met.

When we don't learn healthy models of these concepts, we're more likely to pass on similar models to our own children. While no one wants to alienate themselves completely from their family of origin, it's important to recognize their influence so you can, if nothing else, decide what role your extended family will play in the lives of your nuclear family.

Family of Origin

Allow me to park here for a minute and talk to those of you who may not have experienced the most stellar of upbringings.

First of all, let me tell you that you're not alone. While social media continues to plaster pictures of seemingly perfect families in front of our faces every day, the reality is much less picturesque. If we're struggling with memories of abuse or absenteeism from our own parents (or anything in between), our natural tendency is to swing in the exact opposite direction with our own kids not only in an effort to give them a different experience than we had growing up but in a (usually vain) attempt to knock out our own bad memories in the process.

This concept became increasingly difficult for me to wrestle with after I became a Christian. So much so that when my husband and I sought out marriage counseling to work on some issues we were struggling with, it surprised us just how much time we actually spent talking about our collective families of origin.

And if I may be allowed a pause within a pause, I want to confirm that you heard me correctly: we sought counseling. If you know me, I'm nothing if not transparent. And while I'd like to think I can "fix" everything myself, there came a time and place where we realized we needed some outside professional help.

There is no shame in getting counseling.

There is no weakness in seeking counseling.

There is no stigma in needing counseling.

Did I continue to pray? Yes. Did I continue to work on myself? Of course. But having a wise, experienced third party who could listen to our thoughts, experiences, and stories objectively was and continues to be invaluable for us as a couple, as well as for us as individuals.

One particular illustration that really stood out during the beginning stages with our current counselor (yes, it took a couple of tries to find someone we both clicked with) was that of a brick wall versus a rope fence.

I already mentioned how much time we spent in our sessions discussing the role our respective childhoods played in who we are today, but for some reason, the relationship we had with our extended family still wasn't clear.

So our counselor asked us, "What type of fence have you put between you and your extended family during this time of crisis?"

Confused, we asked him to clarify.

He went on. "Imagine yourselves in your home. Now imagine and describe the fence you've erected that would designate how you're allowing your extended family into your home."

I initially responded by saying I imagined it as a seven-foot solid fence where we couldn't see each other but could still hear each other. My husband, on the other hand, described it as a brick wall going as high as the heavens.

Our counselor quickly called our bluff.

He told us that if we in fact had erected a (symbolic) brick wall between us and our extended family, we would not be allowing the pain, influence, and negative talk we were currently engaging in. Instead, he suggested we had merely put up a rope fence. Sure, it might keep them from driving right in, and they'd have to get out and move the rope first, but it still allowed them in.

Regardless of how you feel about each other, you have to communicate with each other.

At a point where we had been counseled to "take a break" from our extended family to work on putting our own little family back together, you can see where problems would arise. Not only were we "letting them in," the more troubling fact was that we weren't even aware we were doing it.

The point wasn't even whether *all* of our extended family had wronged us, but rather that to move forward as a healthy family and healthy parents, we first had to become a healthy couple made up of two healthy individuals. For that to take place, we had to put a temporary distance between us and our extended family members. The problem was that we didn't adequately communicate that message to them.

Now, I may have lost some of you. You're thinking that you have a great family. You may even live with your extended family because you get along so well. Regardless of how you feel *about* each other, though, you have to communicate *with* each other.

Even in the best scenarios, boundaries must exist and each party needs to be made aware of them. Henry Cloud and John Townsend address this clearly in their book *Boundaries: When to Say Yes, How to Say No to Take Control of Your Life*:

> Boundaries define us. They define what is me and what is not me. A boundary shows me where I end and someone else begins, leading me to a sense of ownership . . . we need to make sure that we are communicating our thoughts to others. Many people think that others should be able to read their minds and know what they want. This leads to frustration. . . . *We have our own thoughts, and if we want others to know them, we must tell them.*[3]

What surprised me to learn about my own mind was that I allowed my sense of justice to stand in the way of my offering forgiveness.

Oswald Chambers summed it up much more eloquently when he said, "Never look for justice in this world, but never cease to give it."[4] Isn't that it in a nutshell? Essentially, he's saying don't seek justice, but never stop extending it. If we're to live this out, and have any chance for our children to do the same, we must learn to be great forgivers.

Stop Fixing

I withheld forgiveness because I'd been wronged, not just with extended family but toward everyone in my life. As the daughter of a lawyer, I'd come to find comfort in rationale and reasoning.

I believed I could talk my way into or out of any situation and always strove to "fix" whatever was wrong.

But as is so often true with matters of the heart, a quick "fix" isn't what most situations call for. In reality, our hearts need healing—and the only One who can offer us that healing is God the Father.

So I stopped the fixing.

First I had to recognize that before I looked to fix anyone else, I had to hold the mirror up to myself. Luke 6:42 doesn't mince words when it warns us:

How can you say to your brother, "Brother, let me take the speck out of your eye," when you yourself fail to see the plank in your own eye? You hypocrite, first take the plank out of your eye, and then you will see clearly to remove the speck from your brother's eye.

After this revelation, it became apparent I had to remove the word *fix* from my vocabulary and instead admit I actually needed *healing* from the heart.

From there, I could begin the road to forgiveness, by asking God to forgive me, by extending forgiveness to myself for the self-inflicted pain and negative beliefs, and then finally by extending it toward those who hurt me.

Let me also be clear and say that the words "I forgive you" need not always be offered to the person who has offended you, especially if the person doesn't realize they committed an offense. In those cases, offering verbal forgiveness may just stir up a new can of worms. Sometimes verbal, face-to-face interactions are necessary to communicate forgiveness and draw a line in the sand, but other times our actions communicate far more than our words ever could.

I can't say I'm fully there yet, nor can I describe this as a "one and done" project. As someone who has suffered from sexual abuse, I know triggers will always emerge that have the potential to stir up old thoughts and emotions. I don't know any potion or

MENTOR MOMENT
RAISING GOOD FORGIVERS

The truth is that I learned forgiveness from one of the best.

You name it, my mentor and spiritual mama, Jackie Kendall, has lived through it (or at least seen someone who has), including everything from abuse to suicide. Yet after coming to know Jesus in high school, she has radically pursued him.

If anyone had the "right" to linger in unforgiveness, it would be this lady. But instead, she not only teaches others how to forgive but practices it in her own life daily. Ultimately, she says one can't love freely without the developed skill of forgiving freely.

In her book *Free Yourself to Love: The Liberating Power of Forgiveness*, Jackie offers so many helpful tips on how to forgive. But there's one concept in particular that speaks specifically to what we're addressing in this book: the concept of honor within forgiveness. This story from Jackie so poignantly illustrates the impact we have on our children when it comes to forgiving others.

> Are you concerned about your children's teeth? If you're like me, you've probably been known to harp on your children to brush and floss their teeth. And it's a good thing to be concerned about! But I am often amazed that parents can be so thorough in teaching their children about dental hygiene yet neglect the ultimate hygiene of the soul. Parents will allow their children to grind their teeth in anger toward a sibling or a teacher or a parent and not get that the soul is actually "cleansed and flossed" when a person learns how to be a good forgiver. . . .
>
> Here are a few coaching tips for teaching your child how to be a good forgiver:
>
> 1. Let the child articulate the grievance, offense or hurt (i.e., being embarrassed by someone in class).
> 2. Ask the child how it made him/her feel. (You are using this situation for healing and instruction in loving freely—which is forgiving freely.)

3. Ask your child to name a "hero." Then encourage her or him to do something truly "heroic"—to forgive this person for hurting their feelings.
4. Encourage your child to pray with you—because to pray for the offending person is to overcome evil with good. Pray that God will bless this person and make him more like Jesus (Rom. 12:21). (Note: You can't fail when you pray with your child. In fact, the only failure in prayer is to not pray.)
5. Remind your child after praying for the offender that this prayer was a most "heroic" act—to pray blessings on those who hurt you is using the "super power" of Jesus in you!

One day our daughter came home crying about how mean her teacher had been the whole week. Apparently there had been several incidents where she had actually screamed at some of the students, including our daughter. I let her continue to share details, so that she could express her difficult feelings, and when she was done I said, "We need to pray for your teacher before you go to sleep tonight." Our daughter said, "We need to pray for her tonight and when we drive into school tomorrow!" . . .

We continued to pray for this teacher, and after a week, the teacher actually wrote a letter of apology to every student. Her private world was in chaos, and she was unfortunately taking her pain out on the students. . . .

These tips on forgiving also apply to mean teens. Some teenagers are so mean they emotionally "eat your child for breakfast" when arriving at school. . . . Praying for the kids who hurt kids is a noble and heroic mission; and, in fact, those mean kids themselves are a critical mission field in our kids' lives.

And remember, as parents, we need to practice these things as much as our children. Being offended is inevitable but staying offended is a choice. A healthy family is a place where failure is not fatal, and where forgiveness is given as freely as hugs and kisses.

Jackie Kendall is one of seven children, has two children of her own, and has three grandchildren. She's been married forty-one years and is a national conference speaker and a bestselling author.

prescription that will forever erase the pain, but I do know the One who holds the power to moving forward. When we can embrace those moments, lay the pain at the foot of the cross, and then graciously look ahead, we retain the essence of who God made us to be instead of believing the lie of the Enemy.

Deuteronomy 5:16 clearly tells us, "Honor your father and your mother, as the LORD your God has commanded you, so that you may live long and that it may go well with you in the land the LORD your God is giving you." But what if your parent abused or abandoned you? How can you honor without subjecting yourself to further abuse or abandonment? And better yet, how do you model forgiveness for your own children if you can't offer it yourself?

Jackie shared with me that "to honor your father and mother is to realize that honor means to consider weight of influence. Is the influence good or is the influence bad? Honor reflects an accurate estimation of a person or object. When one prayerfully estimates the impact of time spent with certain family members, one must limit the toxic exposure."[5]

The essence is this: sometimes our biggest mission field in life is our extended family. Being able to walk through and talk with your children about these scenarios in an age-appropriate way is the best lesson in forgiveness they can ever learn.

Parenting Mirror: Ask in Order to Receive

I'm not sure there's any better way to teach a child about forgiveness than to ask it from them when we've offended them.

Matthew 7:8 reminds us that "everyone who asks receives; the one who seeks finds; and to the one who knocks, the door will be opened."

Let's face it, none of us is perfect, so why do we aspire to be perfect parents? I think the most we can demand of ourselves is to be practicing parents—constantly learning and always striving to become more of who God designed us to be.

I often remind my kids what I heard from God when I came to truly know him and accept him into my life at the age of twenty-five: "Whether people like you or dislike you, they will respect you when you live a consistent life for me."

Are we asked to agree with everyone? No.

Are we called to convert others to our way of thinking? Certainly not.

So why do we think that's what will happen with our children?

I've said it before and I'll say it again: *our example will influence our children far more than our stories ever will.*

Case in point: we do not allow our kids to simply say a less-than-heartfelt "I'm sorry" when they've wronged someone. Instead, we instruct them to not only apologize but then ask forgiveness for the specific act.

We also request that they refrain from shouting to each other from different rooms across the house, but even I have a hard time following that rule.

One time during such a "shouting" match, I thought I overheard my daughter making fun of her brother (something I'd really been getting on her to quit doing). Without emerging from my room, I started yelling back at her, accusing rather than clarifying. My tone obviously communicated to the entire house that I was less than pleased, and my son quickly rushed to his sister's defense, explaining what had really happened.

When our kids (falsely) believe we are perfect as parents, we set up a standard they can never fully measure up to and begin to create a culture of resentment in their hearts.

I knew in that moment I had the opportunity to either rest on my parental laurels or demonstrate the very behavior I required from my own children. I quickly squatted down to my daughter's eye level, admitted I'd been wrong, and asked her to forgive me, not just for what I did but for how I did it (by shouting from another room).

When our kids (falsely) believe we are perfect as parents, we set up a standard they can never fully measure up to and begin to create a culture of resentment in their hearts. When we instead follow through on the standards we set for them, applying them to our own behavior as well, they have the beautiful opportunity to witness a living, breathing example of James 2:22: "You see that his faith and his actions were working together, and his faith was made complete by what he did."

Let It Go

"Bear with each other and forgive one another if any of you has a grievance against someone. Forgive as the Lord forgave you" (Col. 3:13).

Years ago, I lamented over a fairly insignificant issue happening in the apartment complex we lived in at the time. As I lay awake in my bed contemplating whom to call, how they would respond, and what they would do to resolve the issue and prevent it from happening again, I heard something clear as day in my head: let it go.

Mind you, this was years before the infatuating Disney tune by the same name, so it wasn't as though the phrase was constantly swirling in my head like it is these days. Instead, it was as if God was saying, "Excuse me, can I interrupt this nonsense so I can help you get to sleep?"

As soon as I let go that night, a stream of consciousness washed over me and this is what I wrote in the dark on the pad next to my bed:

> Help me to forgive and forget
> help me to let go and be led. . . .

away, by you
from strife to life
from grief to joy.

For no one is as hurt by unforgiveness as me
and no one bears the pain of harbored bitterness but me.

You have paid the price for all my sin and shame,
so who am I to pick it all back up again?

To bear the burden I no longer have to bear alone,
with you,
forgiven and free.

So I say the same thing to you now: let it go. Whatever it may be that's plaguing you, realize that you're punishing no one but yourself and, most likely, your kids as a by-product.

"Forgive as the Lord forgave you" may be easier said than done, but that doesn't mean we have the right to completely give up trying. By first practicing the art of self-forgiveness and then extending that forgiveness to those around you, you give your children the opportunity to witness what it truly means to put feet to their faith. After all, since Jesus paid the ultimate price for our forgiveness, who are we then to deem ourselves or anyone else unforgiveable? Forgiveness may be the first gift we received as Christians, but we shouldn't allow it to be the last gift we extend to those around us, especially our children.

Make It Practical

Of any chapter, you may be thinking this section's suggestion would be the most obvious: go say "I'm sorry" to someone you've wronged. While that may be an important step in your family's forgiveness journey, it shouldnot be the only one. Keep in mind, there may be those whom you just can't bring yourself to forgive, yet they have no idea they've wronged you. So before you run outside your door to put these principles into practice, start in your own heart and then work outward.

- *Burn the bitterness exercise*: Are you holding on to tangible reminders of a person or event that you need to let go of? I'm talking pictures, letters, or the like. Then consider setting them ablaze. This could be as simple as taking a moment alone with the items, a match, and a bucket, or you could turn it into a small ceremony with your friends or family around a campfire or fireplace to make a public declaration of your decision to let the past go and move forward in forgiveness.

- *Speak and share love languages*: You'd be surprised at how many conflicts you can avoid simply by recognizing someone's love language and then speaking to them in that way. Bitterness often arises out of unmet expectations, so by making the effort to become a better communicator, you greatly reduce the chance of offending those you love in the first place!

- *Make things right with those you've wronged*: What if you're not the one to whom an apology is owed, but rather you truly owe someone else an apology? Then do as much as possible in your power to make things right. Hebrews 12:14 challenges us to "make every effort to live in peace with everyone. . . ." Whether this means making a phone call, writing a letter, or taking a trip to reconnect with someone, pray that God will show you what needs to happen to right your heart. Likewise, encourage your children to do the same, keeping in mind that you may need to help little ones come up with ideas and coach them in the implementation.

- *Prayer shield*: I know we are called to cover each other in prayer, but honestly, I'm not the most consistent when it comes to prayer unless I have a plan. A prayer shield allows our family to be intentional about covering those we love in protective prayer on a consistent basis and rallying those same souls to do the same for us.

All you need to do is find someone (friends or a family you know, love, and trust) to commit to praying for your family on the same day of each month. In return, you commit to pray for them and their family on that same day every month.

It's as simple as that. You can send out an email, Facebook message, or phone call asking if friends, family, co-workers, and so on would be interested in committing to do what I described above for one year. That's right, we asked for a twelve-month commitment. I also promised to send out an update at the beginning of each month with what happened in our family in the prior month and what we coveted prayer for in the coming month (something I've not always been consistent with and hope to continue to improve in the coming years).

We then filled out the names of the parties who agreed on a form and posted it in an easily visible, high-traffic area (for us that meant the fridge). I also made smaller copies of the shield to carry in my purse organizer and put in the car.

It's also wonderful to contact the people you're praying for in some way on the day you pray for them. You may not physically be able to get in touch with them each time, but you can't imagine what a simple text message, Facebook post, or quick email will do to brighten your prayer partner's day.

For more practical tips and guidelines, visit SamiCone.com/UncommonKids.

6

WISDOM

Through the Eyes of a Child

If I've said it once to my kids, I've said it a thousand times: you can always find one positive thing in *any* circumstance.

But if I'm being honest, I have to say it's much easier said than done—especially when our very own children get sick or hurt.

Which reminds me, have you ever heard the sound of a barking seal?

Neither had I, until one afternoon when my (then) nineteen-month-old son was up in his crib napping.

Actually, what I heard coming through the baby monitor sounded more like a cat was attacking Britton in the crib. I dropped what I was doing and sprinted up the fifteen steps that stood between me and my baby. To my surprise, the noise was emanating from my own son, not some wild animal.

I snatched him up from his nap and immediately called my pediatrician's office. As I frantically tried to explain the barking noise I'd just heard, he did it again. Without so much as a bit of hesitation, our doctor confidently declared, "He's got the croup; get him to the ER right away."

The croup? Was he serious?

The last and only time I'd heard of the croup was when I used to watch the filmed version of *Anne of Green Gables*, and to be honest, I thought the disease had been wiped out during the same time period the movie was set in.

After all, if this ancient ailment was still around, why hadn't I heard about it? Why didn't any of my mom friends warn me about it? Why wasn't it in the one baby book I actually read?

Questions like these and more raced through my head as I scurried to get a friend to watch my daughter while I rushed my son to the ER.

As soon as we arrived, we weren't made to hang out in a waiting room like one expects; instead, we were immediately ushered back to a hospital bed while I heard a "Code Blue" (or some equally scary color) called out over the intercom.

Before I knew it, two doctors and a multitude of nurses rushed to Britton's side from every angle. While everything within me told me not to take this situation lightly, I couldn't help but imagine what this must look like from my toddler's eyes: the fluorescent lights, the scratchy sheets, the bleeps and blips of the monitors.

Even when life isn't good, God always is.

In less than an hour, he'd been whisked from the familiar and transported into uncharted territory. I remained the only element of normal in an otherwise abnormal experience.

In that moment, I kept my gaze fixed on my son's. Although I couldn't control our current situation, I could remind him of what I knew was true: God's love for us, my love for him, and that he was being cared for in that moment.

Hebrews 13:5 rang more true in my mind that night than it ever had before: "Never will I leave you, never will I forsake you." Even when life isn't good, God always is.

I felt confident from the instant those physicians looked into my baby boy's brown eyes that they would do everything humanly possible to make him well. And they did.

We've had several more hospital visits with our kids over the years: unusual rashes (which turned out to be hand, foot, and mouth disease, another one I'd never heard of before), an exploratory endoscopy, and uncontrollable projectile vomiting, just to name a few. Although every situation was different, one thing remained the same through each incident: my children taught me to see things through new eyes.

When we see things through the eyes of a child, we see things as God truly intended them to be.

In the midst of pain, I found peace.

In the midst of hurt, I found healing.

In the midst of fear, I found faith.

Regardless of what your children may be going through, they will always look to you to know how to respond. Instead of taking their pain upon yourself, why not try to reflect the goodness and hope found so easily in their hearts?

After all, when we see things through the eyes of a child, we see things as God truly intended them to be.

Wisdom, Knowledge, and Understanding

"Let the message of Christ dwell among you richly as you teach and admonish one another with all wisdom through psalms, hymns, and songs from the Spirit" (Col. 3:16).

Wisdom often gets tossed around in sentences among words like knowledge and understanding. Because they are so important to our walk as parents and Christians, let's not confuse them; knowledge may constitute understanding, but wisdom necessitates acting on that understanding.

Wisdom is something that not only needs to be modeled for our children but also, like any skill, needs to be practiced, pondered, and fine-tuned.

If we were to take it one step further, being wise entails exercising restraint and applying common sense and sensitivity to whatever knowledge we possess. Jon Weece, author of *Jesus Prom*, recently spoke at our church and illustrated a similar point beautifully when he said, "If what we believe doesn't affect how we behave, then what's the point?"

But don't take my and Jon's word for it. Look to the Lord. When I search for guidance on wisdom, I typically turn straight to the book of Proverbs. The introduction to Proverbs from my *Hebrew-Greek Key Word Study Bible* explains why so clearly:[1]

> The theme of the book is found in Proverbs 1:7 and 9:10, where it is stated that "the fear of the LORD" is the means by which knowledge and wisdom come. The results of the proper application of wisdom include the ability to use God-given talents wisely, the realization of moral obligations, and both intellectual and spiritual maturity.[2]

Moving through the first four chapters of Proverbs, the chapter headers read (respectively): Exhortations to Embrace Wisdom, Moral Benefits of Wisdom, Further Benefits of Wisdom, and Wisdom Is Supreme. It should come as no surprise that all wisdom and ability have their source in God, but upon further study of the Hebrew word *hokmah* (which wisdom stems from), we learn that wisdom also denotes a sense of skill. If we continue with that line of thinking, wisdom is something that not only needs to be modeled for our children but also, like any skill, needs to be practiced, pondered, and fine-tuned. And while the first place our children need to receive guidance with wisdom is our homes, we'd be naive to believe that's the only place they'll be taught.

One of the first places we learn to trust other adults with the well-being and teaching of our children is the school system. Aside from being at home, kids will spend the largest amount of their time in the classroom. Unless you homeschool your kids, that means you're not only trusting other adults with the care of your children; you're trusting that your children are going to implement the lessons you've been modeling for them in your home.

Why Does She Wear That?

The first week after starting fourth grade at the local public school, Kariss came home asking about a certain girl in her class. At the time, I didn't follow the advice I offer later in the "Make It Practical" section; instead of simply listening to my daughter talk or asking what she needed from me, I immediately launched into fix-it mode.

Worried that she'd heard yet another inappropriate word or, worse, was being bullied, I started asking detailed questions. Instead, Kariss assured me that the classmate in question was kind, but rather she was worried about her. When I asked why, Kariss told me the girl wore the same outfit every day.

She went on to describe how other kids often made fun of her and wondered why she wouldn't just change clothes. As you can imagine, it launched us into a powerful conversation about how her family may not have enough money to buy several outfits each for her and her siblings. But rather than focus on the classmate's financial situation (which Kariss couldn't directly affect), I instead chose to direct our conversation to her classmates' response (which she could affect through her own response).

Sometimes our kids don't see how their one life can ever make a difference in the grand scheme of things, so I broke it down for her this way:

- *Choose your attitude.* The only person we can ever truly change is us. As we've already learned, our actions can often make a much greater impact than what we say. Empower your kids to take responsibility for their own attitude and pray that it will positively influence the attitude of others.
- *Squash the gossip.* Gossip and lies spread like wildfire, especially in school hallways. Another step beyond encouraging our kids to carefully choose their own attitudes is to make sure the gossip stops with them. Coach them on how to respond to classmates who begin to gossip around them, and if that doesn't work after repeated attempts, let them know it's okay to remove themselves from the situation to get help from a trusted adult.
- *Befriend the victim.* When sharing our faith, we never know the impact our testimony can make in the life of another. In the same way, it's difficult to measure the impact we can make on another until we go out of our way to try. Counseling your child to sit with the bullied child at lunch, offer to play with them on the playground, or even just nod at them in the hall can be the small encouragement they need to know they're not alone in this world.

I cannot tell you that my daughter went back to school the next day, led said classmate to Jesus, and now the two are best friends. I can tell you, however, that she returned to school unafraid of the unknown, and instead of running away from the unfamiliar, she engaged in interactions with this classmate, not knowing what might happen as a result. She learned how to walk day by day in God's wisdom through a situation within her own circle of influence.

As I've pointed out already, the book of James is filled with insights on the topic of wisdom, yet perhaps the most practical is James 3:17: "But the wisdom that comes from heaven is first of all pure; then peace-loving, considerate, submissive, full of mercy and good fruit, impartial and sincere." Wisdom is not made up of a single component, but is instead made up of a series of our own worldly experiences contemplated alongside heavenly traits. When we seek God's ways for how to combine the two, especially when it comes to guiding our children, he honors us by illuminating the path ahead. Modeling how to seek God's wisdom and counsel in the same way for your children will benefit them far beyond any words of wisdom you could offer them.

Same Kind of Different as Me

I always want my kids to remember this: what other kids make fun of is actually an opportunity to reach out. I've also seen this firsthand in the university classroom where I teach. I require my public speaking classes to give a personal testimony or family history for their final speech. It's my absolute favorite time of the semester, and I truly believe the classmates learn more from each other by listening to those speeches at the end of the term than they do from me in the months prior.

I teach at a four-year, private, Christian university, but that doesn't mean I don't inevitably hear tales of students emerging from and triumphing over everything from drug addiction and abortions to bullying and eating disorders. But more than hearing what they've learned from their own experiences, I love watching the lights go on in the minds of their classmates. Inevitably, the straight-A student in the front row and the brooding artist in the back row, who otherwise never had reason to talk to each other, all of a sudden realize they share the same struggles.

This beautiful realization came to life on the pages of *Same Kind of Different as Me* through the words of Denver Moore: "I used to spend a lotta time worryin' that I was different from

MENTOR MOMENT
KNOW YOUR VALUES

In a recent phone conversation with Barbara Rainey, I questioned her about the topic of school choice. I knew Barbara had traversed this road with grace and wisdom. Hoping she could shed some light on the new chapter of junior high my daughter was currently struggling over, she shared this with me:

> Be careful not to rush in and rescue your kids. School is simply a vehicle for preparing our kids for later in life. Your goal as a parent is to protect them from evil, guide them in wise biblical thinking, and coach them when they encounter temptation and difficulty. Both over protection and under protection can lead to poor choices in the teen and college years.
>
> Ultimately, you and your husband have to ask yourselves one question: "What is our value system?" By contemplating and praying over the answer, you'll come to understand what you are truly looking for, for your children. Once you do, you can apply what you discover to your school choice for them.
>
> In our family, Dennis and I landed on two specific objectives for our kids in this area: First, we wanted them to relate to kids

other people, even from other homeless folks. I worried that I was so different from them that we wadn't ever gon' have no kind a' future. But I found out everybody's different—the same kind of different as me. We're all just regular folks walkin' down the road God done set in front of us."[3]

Whether your kids are about to start kindergarten or graduate college, the classroom becomes the perfect battleground for fighting against stereotypes—not just in our kids' lives but for us as well. Perhaps you'll discover that you've been asking the wrong questions when it comes to school all along. Instead of wondering about *where* your children should go to school, you should be asking yourself *why* they are going there in the first place. After all, *who* they become isn't simply about *what* they of all races, religions, and socioeconomic levels, because that's what they will face as adults. Second, we wanted them to become leaders for good and to share their faith. As a result of these priorities, we sent our kids to the public school in our county's school system. While many friends sent their children to private, Christian schools, we remained confident in our decision to follow our values. While our children may not have always had lots of strong Christian friends, they learned to embody our family's core values while also walking out their faith in a real-world environment. And when they went to college the abundant temptations held less appeal for them because they had faced similar issues in high school when they could come home and debrief with us. Today our six children, all adults, have kept the faith they were taught as children in our home. They aren't perfect, but they know Who is.[4]

Barbara Rainey is the cofounder of FamilyLife (with her husband, Dennis), a mom of six, Mimi to twenty-one, an author, an artist, an ambassador for Jesus, and the creator of Ever Thine Home.

learn, but the beliefs they internalize and eventually share with those around them.

Parenting Mirror: Field Trip Chaperone

Kids look to you as their parent to reflect goodness and wisdom. For instance, they will witness how you treat others in settings in or related to school, and never is this more evident than on school field trips.

I remember the first time my husband chaperoned a field trip. I participated vicariously by watching via social media throughout that day and loved seeing my boys' smiling faces on Instagram and Twitter. Yet I was shocked to hear a much different response when my husband returned home.

When I asked him how things went, he said he and Britton had a great time, but he was less impressed with the behavior of his fellow chaperones. He was the only dad along for the field trip, which he'd normally have no problem handling, but was disappointed not to be invited into the circle of the moms who were chaperoning. He was reminded of the popular high school cliques and recounted how he found more inclusion from our son's classmates than he did from fellow parents.

And don't think our son didn't notice. Even at his young age, Britton asked my husband several times during the day why the mommies weren't playing with their kids or walking with their class. Even outside of the school walls, we can be an example for how our children should treat others within them.

So how can we help our kids exhibit compassion to peers? By putting into practice everything they've learned at home up until this point and reminding them that regardless of school choice, kids need to be a light in the darkness. That doesn't mean you need to throw them on the mission field at the age of five, but their lives ought to be a light wherever they are. Schools aren't just for children; they're about families and provide a space where kids get to not only practice peer-to-peer relationships but also learn who they want to become as they enter adulthood.

Make It Practical

School is a perfect place for your kids to be creative when it comes to others. Go with them to speak to their principal and teacher to explore ideas. It may be anything from starting their own fundraiser to benefit the school to coming up with ways to serve the school community on an ongoing basis.

Help your kids understand what it means to be a light in the darkness. If they want to do something or go somewhere you're not familiar with, offer to go with them the first time to demonstrate how to behave and respond. Enforce the lesson that we don't need to allow others to bring us down; instead, we can be the light that raises others up.

- *Volunteer at your child's school or in their class*: Getting to know who they're hanging out with, as well as being a physical presence around classmates and teachers, brings your kids comfort and allows them the opportunity to bring some of their examples they've been sharing at home to life.

- *Partner up*: Encourage your kids to find three special friends at school: a peer of similar age they can depend on, a younger or less outgoing child they can be an example to, and an older child they can look up to and ask for help if needed. Knowing other parents in the school can not only help in this process but also make your family more aware of other families you can serve together to help meet their needs.

- *Meet, don't preach*: Become cognizant of meeting your kids' needs in a situation before preaching to them. Listen before speaking, and then ascertain whether they need you to just listen or they need you to help fix a problem. Modeling this behavior will help show them what it means to be a good classmate and a good friend.

- *Unplug*: Don't underestimate the moments when your child first comes home from school. Put down your electronics, get off the phone, and stop whatever you're doing to be fully present with them. Not only will you learn new things about them and their friends, you'll be modeling how they should interact in their own relationships.

For more practical tips and guidelines, visit SamiCone.com/UncommonKids.

7

PATIENCE

Active Restraint

I'm not the most patient driver.

I'd like to think I'm a good driver—and a safe driver at that—but when it comes to patience?

Not so much.

Perhaps it stems back to the fact that I don't have much margin in my life, so I constantly find myself rushing from one place to another. But living in a remote suburban area with only a two-lane road to take me in and out of town has truly challenged this trait in me.

Yet it wasn't until I recently heard my daughter shout out "Come on!" from the backseat when another car pulled out in front of us that I realized my impatience was perhaps rubbing off on my children.

Mainland Mission Trip

Twice a year, our church travels to a little town in Eastern Kentucky. It's a small mining town located in the foothills, where the majority of families receive government assistance.

In 2013, our little family of four made the jump from simply donating toward the mission there and decided to instead make the eight-hour trek up there with our church family.

And I mean trek. I distinctly remember uttering things like this along the way:

> "Surely there's a city closer to home that could use our help?"
>
> "What if we donated our gas money spent on this trip instead of actually coming up here ourselves?"

And the best of all:

> "I feel like we're going to fall off the end of the United States!"

During that half-day car ride, I could not see how what we were doing could possibly be beneficial. Yet this particular trip held multiple means of significance for my husband and me:

- It fell on our tenth wedding anniversary—the first we were celebrating after nearly losing our marriage.
- We were finally going to meet the families we'd been helping virtually through food and gift donations for years.
- Our kids were with us!

That's right, this mainland mission trip was one we embarked upon together as a family. It's rare when a ministry will allow young children to take part in volunteering, much less a multi-day trip. So when we discovered that kids were not only allowed but encouraged to go along, we jumped at the chance to expose our children to a way of living they'd never experienced in their young lives.

But I threatened to ruin any possible lessons the trip could teach them with my attitude during the drive up there.

After my husband reassured me that our minivan was not going to plummet into the ocean if we kept driving east and warned me that despite the fact that the kids were on their third viewing of *Teen Beach Movie*, they could still hear my groans, I took a step back and reevaluated the scenario.

Here I'd been complaining about everything from the drive itself to the roles we'd been assigned once we arrived, when the real purpose of the trip was to share the love embodied within the local church and be the hands and feet of Jesus to those who otherwise might not know the Lord cared about them.

So I readjusted my attitude, slept on the floor in a gym with no air-conditioning, ate unrecognizable lunchmeat for a number of meals, and even served at the back-to-school barbecue we threw by leading the face-painting brigade with zero artistic talent but a multitude of enthusiasm.

But what was even more beautiful to witness was my early-elementary–aged children (who started out shy and concerned because they believed they had nothing of worth to share with this community) learn that their value existed in simply being. They played with the children of the community, offered spare hands when they were needed, and observed that what people lack in resources could be, in part, made up for with love.

My nature to control and organize gave way to patience and participation, with my children's growth a by-product of that gift.

Now whenever the church mentions this town, our kids understand it as not only a mission to give to but a community in which they've lived, even if only for a few days at a time.

Being Second

What we learned as a family from that mission trip, and subsequent trips, has been simple:

Servant leadership means being second.

It's not about rushing to the front of the line, choosing the biggest cookie, or insisting things get done in our own timing. It simply boils down to being patient.

As you can imagine, that's not most children's best quality.

But when you think about it, isn't it easier to teach our children about giving back through patience than through other concepts, like money?

You may not have the opportunity to go on a local mission trip like our family did, but chances are you do have access to a local church where you can put patience to practice.

Shortly after moving to Nashville, we joined Cross Point Community Church, where we have a simple yet profound motto:

Everyone is welcome.
Nobody is perfect.
Anything is possible.

Our pastor, Pete Wilson, models this well, and because he does, we're able to model it for our children. And let me assure you, the people of Cross Point don't simply talk the talk; they walk the walk.

Even though Pete is the founding pastor, he typically introduces himself as just "one of the pastors here" before his weekly sermon. From the outset, Pastor Pete has made it clear that he'd rather have more people reaching out into the community in the name of the church and Christ than claiming to be members and simply taking up seats on Sunday.

The overarching result is that we can accomplish more together than apart.

One of the tangible ways our church has manifested this is through The Dollar Club. Every month, Cross Point asks for everyone in attendance, whether in person or online, to give a single dollar, regardless of whether they typically tithe. That money is then tallied (usually thousands of dollars) and donated to a local charity or family in need without any necessary tie to the church.

The power of seeing how a single dollar can be multiplied when joined with others has made a powerful impact in both the church as a whole and in our children especially. It makes them recognize not only the power of a single dollar, but more importantly, the power of a single individual willing to give.

Parenting Mirror: Putting Patience into Practice

Learning how to celebrate others and trust God's plan is not always the easiest concept to teach our children to embrace, yet it is essential when it comes to putting patience into practice. The truth is that we don't always know who's going to be put into our lives and when we will have the opportunity to help them.

Case in point: One cause that's always been near and dear to my heart has been homelessness. I've always believed it's one area where we can make an immediate impact and influence someone else's life for the better.

Not long after we joined the Bellevue campus of Cross Point, they shared a video during the Sunday morning service about a man who once had "everything" according to the world but lost it all and now was homeless.

> *Learning how to celebrate others and trust God's plan is not always the easiest concept to teach our children to embrace, yet it is essential when it comes to putting patience into practice.*

To my surprise, I found him sitting in the lobby after the service and struck up a conversation with him. I asked how we could help him that day. He simply asked for prayer for himself and his sick girlfriend. I, of course, agreed to pray, but I also asked what else they needed. He shared that they hadn't had breakfast in a while and would appreciate some basics like cereal and bread.

With my two preschoolers in tow, I told him to stay put for an hour and left for a nearby grocery store, where we proceeded to buy several bags of necessities.

When we returned to the church lobby, we found him sipping coffee out of a Styrofoam cup with two other men he shared a tent with near the highway. In my head, I decided there was no way they could make the journey back to their makeshift village with all the groceries in tow, so I quickly offered them a ride.

Before I knew it, the three men squeezed in with my children between their car seats in the back of my minivan and off we went. They guided me onto the highway and the only indication they gave me for where I should drop them off was a Santa hat on the guardrail.

When we spotted the hat, I turned on my blinkers and slowed to a stop on the busy shoulder. They got out, collected the bags, offered their thanks, climbed over the guardrail, and disappeared into the thickets below.

Once my husband returned from work later that day, I proudly shared what had transpired earlier that day and was shocked when he didn't return my excitement! Not only that, he actually chided me for the danger to which he felt I had subjected myself and our children.

Upon further reflection, I came to understand his concerns and realized there in fact could have been a way for me to help these men beyond their immediate need. However, my impulsivity and impatience screamed for me to help them that very second!

As I take the time to reflect back on this instance, I'm honestly not surprised by my actions. I'm one of those people with an entrepreneurial spirit who dreams big (which translates into I'm great at starting projects, but not so good at completing them). While my heart was in the right place for wanting to help the helpless right away, I failed to consider the impact those actions could have on my family, or even those men, in the future.

Colossians 3:12 reminds us, "As God's chosen people, holy and dearly loved, clothe yourselves with compassion, kindness, humility, gentleness and patience." While some people equate patience with passivity, the contrary is actually true in this verse. The Greek word for patience here is *makrothymia*, which in part means self-restraint before proceeding to action. Interestingly enough, it also represents the quality of a person who has power to avenge himself yet refrains from doing so. Rather than sitting back as a bystander in your own life and the lives of others, exercising patience actually requires careful consideration.

If I had simply taken another adult from the church with me or bought them a gift card at the grocery store, I could have met their need while also considering the bigger picture. As caregivers, our patience isn't tested simply in times of trials, but as was the case in my enthusiasm to serve, in times of excitement as well. This doesn't mean celebrating others always has to be premeditated, but we must allow margin in our own lives to trust God's plan.

What you think you don't have time for is perhaps what you need to be making time for the most. Bill Hybels, author of *Too Busy Not to Pray*, says, "Many of us are far too busy for our own spiritual good. . . . Authentic Christians are persons who stand apart from others. Their character seems deeper, their ideas fresher, their spirit softer, their courage greater, their leadership stronger, their concerns wider, their compassion more genuine and their convictions more concrete."[1]

Bill Hybels understands that to be authentic, we need to be uncommon, and that's exactly what our children need to understand too.

Just as it's important to have a plan in place before you start dieting if you hope to succeed, it's equally important to equip yourself and your children for if and when you can't fully meet their needs. Parenting is a marathon, not a sprint. While you may not see the fruits of your labor immediately, rest in knowing that the seeds you plant in your kids today will eventually grow and bloom. Never lament over losing a battle; instead, focus on the goal of the entire campaign and how you want to come out on the other end as a family (and an uncommon one at that!).

Let Go and Let Others

My kids know they can come to me for anything that has to do with math, computers, business, social media, or crazy dance moves. They also know, however, that I won't be able to help them much when it comes to interior decorating, decisions that need to be

MENTOR MOMENT
ALWAYS A PARENT

The important thing to always keep in mind when parenting is that even when you don't know what to do, you know whom you can to turn to; our goal should be to instill that same confidence in our children. Just because our children get older doesn't mean we stop being a parent. Fellow blogger and author Tricia Goyer not only understands this concept fully, but reminds parents of the number one thing any kid wants from their parents, regardless of how old they are.

As long as you are alive, you will always be a parent. I've learned this from my eighty-five-year-old grandmother, who is still doling out a lot of advice and prayers to her daughters, who are in their fifties made quickly, or remembering nonessential facts. All that is totally their dad's territory.

Likewise, I couldn't possibly have all the answers for every obstacle they'll tackle in their teenage years. But chances are I know someone who has more experience than I do in those areas.

The key is to introduce people into your kids' lives early rather than throwing them at them in the midst of their angst.

We first experienced this on a mild level when my daughter was in second grade. Believe it or not, even in her small, private Christian school, there was a lot of girl drama going on. My daughter was unfortunately on the receiving end of a lot of the negativity. Thankfully, Kariss had a wonderful teacher who not only understood her but guided her through that time while still dealing fairly with all involved.

Even after Kariss moved on to third grade, we recognized that the special bond between her and her teacher remained. We saw the inherent value in our daughter having a "big sister" she could turn to and confide in, in having someone besides her parents whom we trusted being a confidante for our girl.

and sixties! With every stage—elementary, teen, and adult—there will be new challenges, but the number one thing a child wants to know is that he or she has a parent who loves, believes in, and will be there for him or her. Isn't that what we all want?

We may not always have the right answers, but we can lead our children to our God, who has the right answers. We can lead them to hope. We can lead them to faith. And even if they refuse to follow our leadership, you can guarantee they will always be watching to see how we do it, even when they don't want to admit it.[2]

Tricia Goyer is a wife, busy mom of six, grandmother of two, blogger, and bestselling author.

As such, we approached this teacher (who at the time didn't have children of her own) and asked if she'd be willing to take our daughter on "dates" occasionally. We'd give her ten or twenty dollars and the two would either grab lunch or just window shop.

We never pushed any agenda on them or treated her like a private investigator, but rather simply encouraged them to enjoy being together. We knew that as their relationship grew stronger, Kariss would one day come to the point where she would stop seeing Ms. D as her teacher and instead seek her as a mentor.

In the years since, we've purposefully sought out other adults (some younger than ourselves and some older) to meet a need in our kids' lives that we couldn't, whether it was an art teacher who could teach Kariss knitting or a trusted neighbor who schooled Britton in the great outdoors.

> *Parents need to be okay with allowing others to speak into their kids' lives.*

It comes down to this: parents need to be okay with allowing others to speak into their kids' lives. Surround your kids with your close friends or trusted acquaintances who can teach them and make up for areas you lack.

Chosen Family

In the last chapter, we looked at our relationship with our extended family, and in this chapter we've explored our church family, but there's one other family group not everyone may have but we cherish: our chosen family.

Our chosen family is those friends who are not blood related, yet we've "adopted" as members of our family through love.

This concept, though not in name, was introduced to me at an early age.

When my parents divorced when I was seven, my mom and I moved in with my "Aunt Joyce," who happened to be my mom's best friend. With the rest of my mom's family either deceased or still in England, Joyce's family took us in as their own: her mom became my grandma (affectionately referred to by everyone who knew her as "Mama Kass"), her siblings became my aunts and uncles, and her niece became my cousin.

There was never any transition, never any weird monikers, and most important, I was never made to feel "less than" compared to their blood relatives. My mom and I were simply grafted into their family.

Because of this model, I learned that it was possible, and even desirable, to redesign what family looked like. After all, none of us may have the ideal family situation. Whether separated by miles or circumstance, the majority of us will find ourselves at some point in in our lifetime in a situation where it's not possible to rely on our families for everything we wish we could rely on them for.

Enter the chosen family.

This shouldn't be too foreign a concept to many of you. After all, I know many a child who refers to his or her parent's best friend as "Aunt" or "Uncle." Rather than entering into a formal agreement with a ceremony attached, we simply live life in an intentional way with certain people whom we love and who in return love us as their own.

One of the reasons we moved to Nashville was so we could do life with one such family. The Lees have been in my husband's life for twenty years, and when we married, I became a part of that bond. My husband and Jeremy were once roommates in their younger years, and now that both are married, our kids (the five of whom are each a year apart) are "cousins."

Now, don't get me wrong. Just like blood families, we don't always see eye to eye on things. But despite our differences, we love each other through them. Not only does my husband now work as a tour manager with Jeremy's wife, Tiffany (aka Plumb, her stage name as a songwriter, recording artist, and performer), but we share most major holidays as well as not so major ones, including milestones in our kids' lives. The Lees have even been known to stand in for Grandparents Day at our kids' school.

After one Thanksgiving together, Tiffany posted this message on Instagram along with a group photo of our two families in front of our Christmas tree:

> A family I am ever thankful for. This is us today with the Cone family. A family that's shared life with us in community the way I believe God intended. We have been friends for 18 years. Ricky (now also my tour manager) @therickcone invited Jeremy to his church @crosspoint.tv the Sunday after we separated on a Tuesday almost 3 years ago. They not only fought like warriors for our marriage . . . they love us the way you pray to be loved by a friend. And brought us to a church that is helping us grow into the people we believe God created us to be. I am especially thankful this year for the Cones and @crosspoint.tv.

Thankfully, I was welcomed with open arms into this chosen family, but I've also been able to extend the invitation to others. While lifelong friends make perfect candidates for such a relationship, don't assume that's the only scenario in which it works. So be on the lookout. You might find chosen family in a neighborhood you serendipitously move into, in a family you bond with in your small group, or even in the parents of your child's best friend. However you meet, the point remains: when you take the time to speak into each other's lives like family, you treat them like you would family.

Community

Even if you don't have a church family or a chosen family just yet, most churches offer a Sunday school class or a community group to plug into.

A community group embraces the heart of what the church should be, yet takes it outside of its four walls. Community groups allow us to come together with other individuals and families to put into action what Christ has called us to.

Community groups are not just about you and your spiritual health, but serve as a model for your kids of what true community in God's kingdom should look like.

As diverse as heaven will be, so should our community groups be. I began by mistakenly believing that my community group needed to be filled with others like me: the same age and life stage as me with kids the same age as mine. Community groups are not just for the purpose of coming together with people you already know, and they're certainly not just about you and your husband making friends. They are truly an opportunity to expose your kids to other families in a safe situation. After all, what better place is there to teach our kids about community and practicing patience than in our own home? It's the perfect example of serving where you live.

I've learned more from my current community group than any other I've been a part of. We range in age from twenty-three to sixty, male and female, single and married. They challenge me to step outside my comfort zone and provide a fresh perspective on any struggles I face. Perhaps most important, my kids see me making time for relationships in a seemingly unconventional way.

We meet on Wednesdays at 8:00 p.m. via Google Hangout. During a time of our lives when I couldn't go out for a group or bring others in my home physically, my church helped me connect virtually with others who had similar constraints. Every Wednesday before my kids go to bed, they know why I'm heading to my office to turn on my webcam. My community group is just one more example of how we can create community even when it doesn't appear to be convenient.

If we end this chapter by looking at Proverbs 19:11, it should come as no surprise that the prior two chapters have led us to this one: "A person's wisdom yields patience; it is to one's glory to overlook an offense."

Forgiveness, wisdom, and patience—all worthy traits in and of themselves, yet so much more powerful when put to work together. In fact, St. Augustine even said, "Patience is the companion of wisdom." The practice of patience is exactly that: a practice. Although your kids may regularly test yours, use that as a reminder to practice patience in your own life so it can spill out into your interactions with them. Only then will your kids truly understand the balance between the steady, even-tempered perseverance and the active, selfless restraint that goes into living a life full of patience.

! Make It Practical

We can learn a great deal about patience, and in turn model it for our children, simply by slowing down. I speak a lot about margin because it's an area in my life I'm continually struggling with and working on. In his book *Margin*, Richard A. Swenson says this:

> Overload is not having time to finish the book you're reading on stress. Margin is having time to read it twice. Overload is fatigue. Margin is energy. Overload is red ink. Margin is black ink. Overload is hurry. Margin is calm. Overload is anxiety. Margin is security. Overload is the disease of our time. Margin is the cure.[3]

Regardless of whether Swenson's examples of overload describe your family, everyone will benefit from putting these principles into practice:

- *Go back to the basics*: Have you ever looked at your entire to-do list and freaked out over everything you have to accomplish in an hour, much less the entire day? Me too. When your patience is running thin, don't forget to go back to the basics: take a deep breath, count to ten, do a yoga pose, make time to laugh—whatever it takes to root yourself in the present moment. This works even better when you can corral your kids to do the same.

- *Serve where you are*: Be willing to serve without recognition. The church is a great place to serve because there is always a need for volunteers and almost always a place for your kids to serve alongside you. Even if you start by serving sporadically, this simple act of walking out your faith with your kids will demonstrate that you don't have to have all the answers to help someone else.

- *Permit your kids to dream*: Strike up conversations with your children about who they would help if they could help anyone at all in the world and how they would help them. While the church provides a wonderful vehicle and means to help others, don't limit your children to only the opportunities in front of them. But do recognize that any great plan needs time to develop and the dream to get started.

- *Practice the presence of people*: Pastor Lance Witt introduced me to this concept in his book *Replenish: Leading from a Healthy Soul*.[4] If God called us to be in relationship, why then do we often get so annoyed by others? A lack of patience can often point to a disconnect in our relationship with God. The minute you begin to feel this way, or notice this trend in your children, jump back into God's Word and purpose to stay relationally connected to those around you.

- *Send a letter or note to someone who needs encouragement*: Regardless of how old your kids are, most can write, draw, or help with a note. Most churches have a "card ministry," where volunteers send notes with congratulations, condolences, and, of course, thanks to their members. This is a simple way to serve others *with* your family from *within* your own home. You can take this a step further by praying over the individuals you're sending the cards to as you prepare them.

For more practical tips and guidelines, visit
SamiCone.com/UncommonKids.

8

KINDNESS

The Need Next Door

At the height of the seller's real estate market in the summer of 2005, we decided to sell our townhouse. Our daughter was one and I was pregnant with our second child. With our projected earnings on the sale, not only could we pay off the mortgage on our Florida home, but we'd be in a position to pay cash in full for a modest home in Tennessee.

As fall approached, we moved forward with our plan, which led me to resign my position at the university where I taught and my husband to request a job transfer.

Then it happened. The contract on our home fell through. Then another fell through, and eventually a third contract failed too. By this point I was eight months pregnant and fairly certain I couldn't move even if I'd wanted to.

Within months, we went from potentially being in the most secure financial situation of our married life to the most devastating.

Instead of being debt free, we now faced losing everything. Where we had been barely making ends meet on two small salaries, we were now faced with living on my husband's Starbucks salary alone. Realizing we had no choice but to stay put, we sold everything we could, including our second car, and realigned our priorities.

Hurricane Frances

Though it seemed things couldn't get worse, we soon found ourselves bracing for a major hurricane. After the storm passed and the power went out, all our Florida neighbors gradually gathered in the center of our street to assess the damage. While we discovered a lot of debris and structural damage, no one had been hurt. But more than that, we discovered that if we pooled all our resources, we were not only going to get by, we could flourish!

Before we knew it, those of us with gas grills had dragged them out into the middle of the street, forming a makeshift prep kitchen. We all emptied our fridges and grilled all the meat and vegetables we had. We took turns sharing generators to assess damage and provide necessary power, even if only for an hour at a time.

When morning came, we headed back to the center of the street for a "grilled" breakfast of eggs, bacon, sausage, and yes, even coffee for those who wanted it. We pulled out lawn chairs, turned on battery-powered radios, and waited for news of relief.

That scene repeated itself for the next three days, and during that time we did more than share resources with neighbors; we made new friends.

We discovered new neighbors who were expecting their second child too, due just weeks before ours. The wife moved to our street in particular because her brother and his wife, who also had a young daughter, already lived there, and we all became friends. Once the wreckage from the storm was cleared, we started our new life, but now with new friends going through similar struggles and life stages as us.

The three of us moms, all without jobs due to different circumstances, met on the street nearly every morning. We joked that our double strollers were our cars, and instead of lamenting that fact, counted ourselves blessed that within a mile radius we could walk to a bank, grocery store, bookstore, shoe store, Walmart, and even the Starbucks where my husband worked.

We typically ventured out for a walk together every morning from that point forward, and always seemed to end up at the grocery store to get our kids a free balloon and cookie. Can you picture the three of us each with our double strollers with balloons tied on and kids hanging out from every angle? People would honk and wave as we navigated the side streets, thinking we were putting on a makeshift parade. We may not have known how we were going to make ends meet on a day-to-day basis, but we did know we could rely on God to help us get through those tough times.

Lessons Next Door

Our circumstances literally forced us to get out of our comfort zone; we had to walk out our front door and into our neighborhood for help during the aftermath of the hurricane, and because of that, we not only developed new friendships, but learned something new from everyone around us:

- Perseverance from the single moms living on either side of us
- Consistency from the veteran across the street
- Hospitality from the adopted grandparents a few houses down
- Adaptability from the immigrant kitty-corner from us
- Creativity, flexibility, and genuine kindness from the two couples we now shared life with daily

When we gave our neighbors a glimpse into our own lives, they allowed us to glimpse into theirs. And as we learned lessons from each of them through simple observation, we also discovered their individual needs and how we could help.

Even as toddlers, our children got to witness firsthand the joy that the grandparents at the end of the street got when we'd knock on their door just to say hi or go inside to play with the toys they had saved for their own grandchildren when they came for a rare visit.

They heard the accent of someone different from them and stories about what it took to transition to life in a new country.

They witnessed "Cowboy" on his daily walk and the consistency of his actions, even when his words were few.

I'm convinced in those early years when they themselves could barely form their own sentences, my children observed what kindness was with their eyes before we could ever define it for them with our words.

How to Be a Good Neighbor

In Matthew 22, Jesus was asked which is the greatest commandment in the Law. He replied with this in verses 37–40: "'Love the Lord your God with all your heart and with all your soul and with all your mind.' This is the first and greatest commandment. And the second is like it: 'Love your neighbor as yourself.' All the Law and the Prophets hang on these two commandments."

While most Christians don't debate the "first and greatest commandment," the second prompts a bit more discussion. When Jesus says, "And the second is like it," he implies that the second must flow from the first, meaning we cannot have one without the other: to love God is to love your neighbor and vice versa. It's also interesting that Jesus instructs us to "love your neighbor as yourself," implying that we first must comprehend and practice self-love before we can share love with others.

I'm hoping that by this point in our journey together you not only understand what it is to love, but you're practicing it on others and yourself. What still remains unclear, however, is who exactly is our neighbor. Does Jesus literally mean the person in the house next to us or is the term meant to represent another population entirely?

To discover the answer, I once again dug into my *Hebrew-Greek Key Word Study Bible*. In Matthew 22:39, the Greek word for neighbor is *plesion*, which is also used in its counterpart verse in Mark 12:33, as well as in the parable of the good Samaritan found in Luke 10:29. By studying this word's origin, we discover that "anyone within close proximity to us should be the object of our concern, regardless of whether or not there are mutual ties of kindred or nation."[1]

So, technically speaking, our "neighbor" not only lives next door but is the person near us wherever we find ourselves. Applying that knowledge means that our opportunities for outreach immediately multiply. But before we get ahead of ourselves, let's start in our neighborhood.

Parenting Mirror: Look Both Ways

When our kids are babies, they meet milestones on their own schedule: the first time they sleep through the night, the first time they roll over, the first time they eat solid food, and yes, even their first word. But as our kids grow, we help determine those milestones: when they can stay home by themselves, when they get their own phone, and when they are old enough to date (gasp!). The later set of milestones can be so difficult to determine because not only are all kids different, but you also need to consider external factors beyond your child's developmental stage.

I still vividly remember one such milestone when my kids were in the early elementary school years. We'd just bought our first house in Nashville (yes, the one far from concrete that I told you about in chapter one), which happened to be down the road from one of Britton's classmates and around the corner from his kindergarten teacher and good friends of ours from church. Suffice it to say, we landed in a friendly neighborhood.

Once we recognize and put an end to parenting in fear, we begin to pave the way to truly preparing our family to be good neighbors.

Still, the idea of letting my children play outside alone was a foreign one to me after living in an apartment for so long, much less letting them wander the neighborhood on their own. I wanted to allow them the freedom to explore, but somehow I always let fear get in the way.

I can't tell you exactly what prompted the question, but one beautiful Saturday afternoon my kids asked

MENTOR MOMENT
OBSERVING THE NEED NEXT DOOR

Just like we cannot handpick our kids' teachers, coaches, and so on, we also cannot handpick our neighbors. While we may not develop a deep relationship with everyone around us, we should open our eyes to the needs next door. Friend and mentor Cindy Easley shared an instance where a simple act of observation led to a kind act that eventually turned into a sweet relationship.

When we first moved to Chicago, our next door neighbor was an elderly woman in her seventies who lived in a tiny little house. We seldom saw her, at least not much more than a quick wave when she pulled into her driveway and walked the few steps into her home. Her adult son also lived with her. We would see him occasionally as well, usually mowing the lawn or doing another quick outdoor chore.

Winter hit (as it does in Chicago), and because snow is not a reason to stop life in the Midwest, I would wake my kids in the if they could walk down to their friend's house at the end of the street by themselves. A moment of panic crept over me, as I was not sure if I was ready to let them make this leap. But I knew they'd been making good choices and had demonstrated they could be trusted, especially when it came to looking out for each other.

I reluctantly agreed, and as they walked out the front door, I followed behind them. They quickly stopped me on the porch, saying they didn't want me to even walk them to the end of the sidewalk. I sat myself on the porch and watched them walk over the small hill that would eventually lead them to the safety of their friend's house. (I may or may not have texted their friend's mom as soon as they were out of my sight to make sure she kept an eye out for them.) Not only did they get there safely, but I wish you could have seen the smiles on their faces when they came walking back home to me, once again on their own.

morning to help me shovel snow off our driveway and sidewalks before I took them to school. A couple of days went by and I noticed that our neighbor's drive was still covered in snow. That morning I asked my elementary-aged kids to also shovel her driveway and sidewalk. With a few groans and a little push back, they did. About the time they finished, the neighbor stuck her head out her door. She was overwhelmed. Her son was in the hospital recovering from a heart attack. She had been taking a taxi to visit him because she couldn't get her car out of the driveway with the heavy snow accumulation.

No one had ever helped her that way before. Needless to say, my kids shoveled the drive for the next few months and we had a sweet relationship with that woman until we moved.[2]

Cindy Easley is a mother of four, the author of *Dancing with the One You Love*, a realtor, and the wife of Michael J. Easley, teaching pastor of Fellowship Bible in Nashville and former president of Moody Bible Institute.

As parents, we must walk a fine line between preparing or protecting our children and actually scaring them. I knew that no matter how much I might try to boost their confidence, if I harbored my own fears they would sense it and my entire verbal message would be useless. That's when I remembered 1 John 4:18: "There is no fear in love. But perfect love drives out fear, because fear has to do with punishment."

The moment we allow fear to consistently creep into our conversations with our kids, manipulation inevitably follows. Yet once we recognize and put an end to parenting in fear, we begin to pave the way to truly preparing our family to be good neighbors.

Where You Go I'll Go

Wherever we may find ourselves in life, I can assure you it's not by accident. And even the most unusual circumstances or surroundings can offer an opportunity for you and your family to demonstrate kindness.

One of my favorite books of the Bible demonstrates this neighborly love exquisitely. In the first chapter of Ruth, we find a woman, Naomi, and her two daughters-in-law have all become widows. While custom dictates that Ruth and Orpah return to Naomi's homeland with her, Naomi says to them, "Go back, each of you, to your mother's home. May the LORD show you kindness, as you have shown kindness to your dead husbands and to me. May the LORD grant that each of you will find rest in the home of another husband" (Ruth 1:8–9).

Even the most unusual circumstances or surroundings can offer an opportunity for you and your family to demonstrate kindness.

While Orpah went back to her people, Ruth "clung to" Naomi (1:14). Then in verse 16, Ruth begins a sentiment so kind, so beautiful, so touching that it has become an anthem everywhere from weddings to modern songs:

> Don't urge me to leave you or to turn back from you. Where you go I will go, and where you stay I will stay. Your people will be my people and your God my God. Where you die I will die, and there I will be buried. May the LORD deal with me, be it ever so severely, if even death separates you and me. (Ruth 1:16–17)

Because of that pledge, Ruth returned with Naomi (soon to become Mara) to Bethlehem and became the recipient of a kindness at the hand of Boaz, her kinsman-redeemer, like she'd never before experienced. Boaz and Ruth would eventually marry and become the great-grandparents of King David.

Naomi was a good neighbor to Ruth, Ruth was a good neighbor to Naomi, and Boaz was a good neighbor to them both. Each put the other's needs above their own at different points in their story, and while I'd venture to say none of their lives turned out the way they may have initially imagined, God truly redeemed all their stories. Their love story perfectly demonstrates that God's kingdom consists of one big neighborhood.

Make It Practical

One verse that immediately comes to mind when I think of kindness is "Be kind and loving to each other" (Eph. 4:32 NCV). In fact, we have a tune that goes with it that helped the kids memorize it when they were itty-bitty. But knowing to be kind and acting on it are two very different things.

Modeling kindness for our kids and then involving them in kind acts with us is so important to help them cultivate eyes that see the needs around them, wherever they may be. Here are just a few suggestions for helping your family practice kindness in your neighborhood:

- *Perform random acts of kindness*: We've all heard the term "random acts of kindness," but now is your opportunity to make them come alive for your kids. Start in your home by demonstrating what it means to help others without expecting anything in return and then move outside your walls. When you're in the car with your kids, strike up a conversation while driving through the neighborhood about who they'd like to help and how they'd like to do it. Depending on your kids' ages, this can be anything from literally knocking on a neighbor's door and asking if they need help around the house to cleaning up common areas in your neighborhood.

- *Become visible*: One of the best ways to get to know your neighbors is to make yourself and your family visible. Obviously, this is easier during some times of the year than others, but make a point to spend time outside—sitting on the front porch, playing basketball with your kids on the driveway, or even just walking around the neighborhood. You can't expect to meet the needs of your neighbors until you actually meet them!

- *Bake and take*: Neighbors may already be used to having kids ring the doorbell to sell them fund-raising items, but have you ever considered showing up on their doorstep simply to give them a gift? I love getting in the kitchen with my kiddos, but honestly, we don't need to eat everything we bake. So when we can bless someone else with a homemade treat, it gives us the joy of spending time baking together and then blesses someone else with an unexpected gift.

- *Sell and give*: I'm always up for a garage sale. Seriously. I can't remember a time I've ever declined when a friend or neighbor asked if I wanted to join forces on a garage sale. In fact, I've even woken up on a Saturday morning to find a garage sale going on in our neighborhood and thrown some things out onto our driveway to take advantage of the traffic! That being said, I truly love garage sales for multiple reasons:

1. They clean out the clutter. Our family has a rule: if something new comes into the house, something old has to go out. So we're always collecting items for a potential garage or consignment sale.

2. They reinforce for our children that everything has value and that if you're not willing to take care of something you will lose it. Having frequent garage sales also provides tangible moments for us as parents to point our kids back to when they do want to make an impulse buy in the store. That pause helps them reflect on whether it's really worth it to spend their cash. Which brings me to point number 3 . . .

3. They bring in extra money. It's great to turn a few hours on a Saturday into hundreds of dollars. We not only require the kids to help in the process, but allow them to set up their own tables to sell from. They've created everything from homemade coloring books, art, and bracelets to sell to a "grab bag pile," where they allow kids to fill up a lunch sack of small toys and figurines for a dollar. Once they see how hard they have to work for their profits, it gives them a better perspective when it comes to spending, saving, and giving.

4. They create community. Finally, I love garage sales for the community they create. Sitting outside for several hours, you inevitably see most of your neighbors, whether they're coming by to shop or driving by on their way to work or to run errands. Again, it sets up a visual reminder that you're a part of the neighborhood. I also love meeting new people. I truly believe God always sends someone to our garage sales, not for the sake of shopping but for the sake of sharing. The conversations that take place

never cease to amaze me, and I dare say we've ended up giving as much away as we've ended up selling as a result. I still remember the faces of the pregnant military wife whose husband had been deployed, the young child fighting cancer, and the grandma who wanted to stock her playroom even though her daughter had yet to allow her grandchild to come for a visit. I could never have scripted those encounters and the impact they made on our entire family. Check out my seven favorite tips for how to organize a successful garage sale here: http://samicone.com/how-to-organize-a-successful-garage-sale/.

For more practical tips and guidelines, visit SamiCone.com/UncommonKids.

YOUR INFLUENCE IN THE WORLD

We've examined our children's hearts at home, we've established a proper attitude toward others, and now it's time to cultivate their influence in the world.

The final step in our three-pronged approach is to take what we've modeled for our children and aim it toward our city, state, country, and, ultimately, the world.

Just as we couldn't begin expecting our children to be world-changers before first starting with focusing their hearts on God, we can no longer expect our children to remain idle when they now understand the impact they can make outside their own homes.

I once heard that we can't expect to influence the world by being like it. By definition alone, according to the Oxford Dictionaries, influence denotes "the capacity to have an effect on the character, development, or behavior of someone or something, or the effect itself."[1] Just as I pray a shift is taking place in your family as you progress through each biblical trait discussed in Colossians 3, so too must we use that internal transformation to bring change for the better around us.

And please hear me when I say "bring change." Your responsibility may not be to accomplish the change itself, but merely to act as a change agent to challenge the status quo.

Whenever I begin to feel insignificant or doubt my place in God's plan, I reread 1 Corinthians 3:5–9:

> What, after all, is Apollos? And what is Paul? Only servants, through whom you came to believe—as the Lord has assigned to each his task. *I planted the seed, Apollos watered it, but God has been making it grow.* So neither the one who plants nor the one who waters is anything, but only God, who makes things grow. The one who plants and the one who waters have one purpose, and they will each be rewarded according to their own labor. For we are co-workers in God's service; you are God's field, God's building. (emphasis added)

Ultimately, it's God who will accomplish his purposes through us, but we are all co-laborers in his kingdom. The very first entire chapter of the Bible I ever memorized was Ephesians 4, which starts by echoing the message in 1 Corinthians:

> As a prisoner for the Lord, then, I urge you to live a life worthy of the calling you have received . . . There is one body and one Spirit, just as you were called to one hope when you were called . . . So Christ himself gave the apostles, the prophets, the evangelists, the pastors and teachers, to equip his people for works of service, so that the body of Christ may be built up. (Eph. 4:1, 4–5, 11–12)

God has placed a unique calling on each and every one of our lives, equipping us with unique talents and abilities to carry those callings out through him. The question is, are you ready to answer the call?

In the final four chapters, we'll look at the characteristics of gratitude, peace, humility, and compassion to discover how our children can create a new reality, not just in their own lives but in their city, state, and country, and eventually throughout the world.

9

GRATITUDE

Kids Can Too

Every fall when the weather starts cooling down and the leaves start changing color, we get extra excited here in the Cone home.

We were made for this weather.

We can't understand why anyone would want to live anywhere other than the mid-South in the fall, where the day starts with clear blue skies and the temperature graces the 50-degree mark.

And for whatever reason, it seems that every year as the temperatures drop, the idea of volunteering comes up.

Perhaps it's because autumn signifies the start of the holiday season and cold weather, two reasons that make it even more unbearable for many of us to imagine others alone and without basic needs being met. There is a whole world out there that we desperately want to expose our children to so they don't get too comfortable in their own surroundings. Part of the natural battle comes in making the unknown more tangible to them.

While it can be hard for them to fully relate to the sights, smells, and conditions of the less fortunate living in the city around them, it isn't hard for them to relate to other children. But before you throw your kids into a "trial by fire" volunteer experience, helping them understand where they come from will better equip them to relate to others by finding a common ground. Sometimes you only have to look as far as your own ancestry to discover the key to unlocking gratitude in your own family.

Diversity in My Home

Though I was born and raised in America, I experienced more cultural diversity than the majority of my schoolmates.

I already shared that my mom hails from England, and though my dad was born in the United States, his mother was born in Kiev (Ukraine) in the late 1800s and his dad was born in what's now considered Poland (though due to border shifts it was considered part of Hungary at one point in history). A first-generation American, my father was born during the height of the Great Depression in Chicago and fought in World War II.

To imagine such an upbringing wouldn't affect a child would be naive. Honestly, I don't stand a chance of instilling in my kids the kind of gratitude and appreciation that came to my parents naturally from growing up in that era.

Today, we give kids "jobs" to do around the house in an effort to make them appreciate all that's been given to them. In my father's youth, he had to work outside the home as a young boy to help his family make ends meet. In fact, he recalls there wasn't one day from the time he was eight years old that he didn't work. When he was just twelve years old, he ran a newspaper stand on a corner two blocks from his home in the heart of Chicago.

At thirteen, he'd ride his bike about four miles from his house to a barbecue place, where he served curbside.

By sixteen, he went to work at the Stevens Hotel (taken over by the Air Force in WWII) as a soda jerk for the airmen who were housed in their 3,300 rooms. Not long after that, he became the chief typist for the clerk engineer. He left school at 3:00 p.m. each day and worked from 4:00 p.m. to midnight. After getting out of the service in 1946 at the age of twenty, he went to college for two years and then immediately into law school for three years—all of which was paid for by the GI Bill.

Take Nothing for Granted

It's not to say that young people today don't ever work for what they have, but motivation and consequences are glaringly different from the past century. In her article "Volunteering: Service Brings Gratitude, Happiness, Appreciation, Love," Stephanie Hamlow further describes this dangerous trend in our youth:

> It is important that people start volunteering at a young age. There has been a growing sense of entitlement in our society. I have witnessed teens and young adults proclaim their worthiness and expectations of having the best of everything without having to earn it. I have watched parents give their children items and privileges with limited expectations of "good behavior" or "good grades."[1]

Though I stopped living with my father at the age of seven, the impact of his upbringing continued to be passed on to me whenever we spoke or saw each other: nothing was taken for granted, the next meal was never assumed, education was a gift, and the work ethic was unparalleled.

Children in his era recognized that their parents made supreme sacrifices for a chance to give their children a better life, often leaving their home country and extended family behind. So they worked alongside each other accordingly.

Am I suggesting we return to such times? No, but I am suggesting that we must learn from them. I could insert a bevy of quotes on studying history here, from along the lines of "We must study history or we're doomed to repeat it" to one of my favorites from the film *My Big Fat Greek Wedding*: "Don't let your past dictate who you are, but let it be part of who you will become."[2] And while both sentiments may be true, none will guide us as accurately or poignantly as the Word of God when trying to find the right balance of gratitude and discipline in our families.

> *When we feel as though we have nothing to give, we can always offer up our gratitude.*

Psalm 50:14–15 reminds us where we need to start with any type of service and sacrifice: "Sacrifice thank offerings to God, fulfill your vows to the Most High, and call on me in the day of trouble; I will deliver you, and you will honor me."

When we feel as though we have nothing to give, we can always offer up our gratitude. In fact, thankfulness is at the root of raising uncommon kids. "Thank offerings" in this verse comes from the Hebrew word *todah*, which comes from *yadah*, meaning "to boast and praise." More specifically, this term denotes offering praise to God as a sacrifice.[3]

Before we can ever expect our kids to help others, they first need to exhibit gratitude for what they have.

And I'm not just talking about material things.

The life God has blessed us with and called us to is reason enough for offering up thanks to God. By acting as our children's tour guide through life, helping to point out the many miracles that pass in front of us each day, we begin to demonstrate the power of gratitude.

The Greater Good Science Center at UC-Berkeley compiled recent research on gratitude in our kids and discuss it on their website:

> Results suggest that gratitude not only helps people form, maintain, and strengthen supportive relationships, but it also helps people feel connected to a caring community.
>
> Evidence from our own research suggests that grateful young adolescents (ages 11–13), compared to their less grateful counterparts, are happier and more optimistic, have better social support, are more satisfied with their school, family, community, friends, and themselves, and give more emotional support to others. We've also found that grateful teens (ages 14–19) are more satisfied with their lives, use their strengths to better their community, are more engaged in their schoolwork and hobbies, have higher grades, and are less envious, depressed, and materialistic.[4]

Of course, while an attitude of gratitude can start within our own homes and hearts, we must also begin to introduce our children to the role having a thankful heart plays in making visible change in the world around them.

Where to Start

While our parents' generation may have been motivated to work and serve out of necessity, our children need to be inspired in different ways.

The best thing we can do is meet our kids where they are and start there.

The truth is that our original motivation was urged on by free Disney World tickets.

When our kids were just preschoolers, we got serious about finding opportunities where our kids could volunteer too. It just so happened that Disney World was offering free tickets if you volunteered for a day. But what was really great about their website was that they were clear in presenting opportunities where kids could participate as well.

That's how we found out about Good Food for Good People in partnering with Hands on Nashville. Every week this organization would gather at a local church to provide a healthy, homemade meal for the homeless.

It didn't take us long to be welcomed in by the organization. On the appointed Thursday, we showed up at the small church. Our kids played in the neighboring nursery room while we prepped and cooked food, and then they came in to eat and fellowship with us as a group. Once all the food was served, they grabbed sponges and buckets to help clean up.

MENTOR MOMENT
LIVE TO GIVE

We all think our children are special, but making them feel unique without letting it go to their heads can be challenging for any parent, much less one with multiple children in the public eye. Friend and mentor Barbara Cameron understands this dilemma all too well, so I knew she would be the perfect mentor to offer advice on this topic.

During the years of *Growing Pains* and *Full House*, I remember how important it was to teach our children [actors Candace Cameron Bure and Kirk Cameron] that just because they were on TV they weren't any different than other children.

Production would hire extras to come in to do scenes and separate them from the main cast. It used to bother me, as though we were different or we were supposed to be more privileged than they were.

It was important to teach my children that they were not any more special than anyone else. They had a job and they were to respect and be polite to everyone on the set, even the extras.

I would also do the same. Many times the parents of the cast would sit in their children's dressing rooms, and the extra children's parents would sit in the bleachers. Well, if I was to be an example to my children I needed to do the same.

Even though our kids weren't actually chopping or cooking the food, they still got to help, and more important, they got to meet the people being directly affected by the organization.

Kids in Need

As you'll come to read in the last chapter, the one thing that enlightened my children to others in need more than anything else was discovering other kids in need.

After that initial volunteer experience, we continued serving every Thursday night we could as a family. Somewhere toward

I sat in the bleachers making wonderful friends and having great conversations, sharing with them that not all child actors were any more special than their children and that not all moms were "stage moms."

There were also the times during the holidays that it was important for me to make sure that our children gave back to those who were in the hospitals or orphanages.

These children would be confined to their hospital rooms and watch TV all day long. They were fans of the shows, and for some of the cast to come to see them was a dream come true! It put smiles on their faces that were priceless! Can you imagine having the privilege of giving back just by stopping by a hospital bed to put a smile on a child's face?!

That is what it truly was for me and for me to teach our children.

Today both of my children serve those in need, and I believe it is because of what they learned and experienced during those years of *Growing Pains* and *Full House* with the platform that God gave them.

"Just as the Son of Man did not come to be served, but to serve, and to give His life a ransom for many" (Matt. 20:28 NKJV).[5]

Barbara Cameron is an author, speaker, talent agent, wife of forty-five years, mother of four, and grandmother of sixteen.

the end of that first month, our kids saw something that shocked them: homeless kids.

For whatever reason, my little ones hadn't connected with the fact that kids could be homeless too. As you can imagine, seeing a homeless woman come in with her two young children prompted a plethora of questions from their spinning minds.

"What are kids doing here?"

"Do they have to sleep on the street?"

"Why isn't their mom doing something about it?"

"Can we take them home?"

Some may think their comments ignorant; I simply see them as a reflection of our human nature, which is even more reason why we need to train our kids in the way they should go and when they are old they will not depart from it (Prov. 22:6).

While of course it broke my heart to see these little ones who played no part in their fate, it troubled me just as much that I'd exposed my children to a situation that seemed to have no immediate solution.

Instead of letting the scenario depress and overwhelm us, I purposed to brainstorm with my kids on how we could become part of the solution rather than allowing the problem to perpetuate. Too many people allow the feeling that their individual efforts won't make a dent in the bigger problem to keep them from taking any action at all. Instead, I wanted my children to see that if each of us took just one step toward change, we in fact could make a difference much sooner than anyone could ever imagine.

Parenting Mirror: How Others Live

"Let the message of Christ dwell among you richly as you teach and admonish one another with all wisdom through psalms, hymns, and songs from the Spirit, singing to God with gratitude in your hearts" (Col. 3:16).

It's not enough to expose your children to how others live around them; it's up to you as their parent to partner with them to discover ways they can lend a hand. In the same way, it's not enough for us as individuals to expose ourselves and our children to the words of Christ; we must make room for Christ to live in our lives and our hearts. I'm not just talking about unwelcome houseguests or long-lost relatives who invite themselves over occasionally as they're passing through town. No way.

> *It's not enough to expose your children to how others live around them; it's up to you as their parent to partner with them to discover ways they can lend a hand.*

What I'm talking about is a relationship where Christ's mind and heart encompasses ours rather than our trying to make it the other way around. Too often, we try to fit God's ways into our lives instead of our lives into his ways. Whenever I recognize this symptom in my own life or my children's lives, I'm reminded of Isaiah 55:8–9:

> "For my thoughts are not your thoughts,
>   neither are your ways my ways," declares the LORD.
> "As the heavens are higher than the earth,
>   so are my ways higher than your ways
>   and my thoughts than your thoughts."

To truly recognize God's presence in our lives, we need to speak his language. The only way we can do this is by reading his Word. I'm not talking about only devotionals, commentaries, and topical studies (though all are valuable accompaniments). I mean the Bible itself. If your kids are too little to read for themselves, pray over them or read the Bible to them. If your younger kids are intimidated by picking up the Bible, read it with them or help them memorize Scripture. If older children don't show interest in picking up the Bible, practice your memory verses out loud so the vocabulary naturally becomes a part of your everyday conversations.

One of the reasons we started praying Scripture over our kids as soon as they were born was so they'd be familiar with God's Word. In essence, we treated it just like we would any new language we wanted to teach our kids. Research has shown that young children are much more able to learn foreign languages, and I've seen this exhibited in my children firsthand.

Whenever people question this principle, I always refer to students taking a foreign language in high school for the first time. There's a marked difference between students who have previously been exposed to a foreign language and those who are hearing the sounds for the first time. Even if someone has never learned to speak a word of their nonnative language, any previous experience with it can markedly increase their ability to learn it.

Exposing our children to God's Word works in much the same way. Before we can expect Christ to dwell in us, we must recognize his Word and his ways. This means continual and repeated interactions with the Father of all creation.

Once we've primed our lives for such experiences through our knowledge of his Word, we're truly able to live out the exhortations of Colossians 3:16 and, more important, guide our children in doing the same.

Step toward Change

The most important step to take toward change is to have a dialogue with your kids. (Notice I say "dialogue" and not "speech," the latter meaning just talking at them.) Discuss why it's important to give of our time and gifts (both intrinsic and financial), discover what they're passionate about, and build a volunteer experience from there. If they love animals, look at visiting a local shelter and walking the animals. If they love art, call your local art museum and find out if they can help with cleaning up the kids' areas there. If they love kids, maybe they can volunteer at your church nursery.

Kids' volunteer possibilities are endless; you just have to start somewhere, regardless of how old your children are. Even when your kids may seem too young to participate in the volunteer activity itself, you'd be amazed to discover the benefit of having them with you while you volunteer in your own city.

The Nashville Flood of 2010

We lived in three homes within our first twelve months of moving to Nashville. Never did we imagine we'd have to uproot our family so many times in such a short period.

And then the flood hit.

In 2010, Nashville experienced the most devastating flood in over a century. Entire communities were submerged, and people all around us had to be rescued from their homes by boat. And it goes without saying that we spent days and weeks without the modern conveniences we'd come to rely upon so heavily.

At the time we couldn't see why everything happened to us the way it did, but then we learned the other two places we lived in and had to leave in the nine months prior had flooded.

You can imagine how quickly the bitterness I'd harbored gave way to gratitude for our little apartment on the hill.

But I wasn't alone in gratitude. Amid the destruction and even death that resulted from this disaster, our city rallied to help each other. Even with a lack of national media coverage, the people of Nashville put their own needs aside to help others who couldn't help themselves.

As the mom of two preschoolers, I felt bad that I didn't have a way to get in the trenches and help; after all, the majority of work in those early days involved activity like tearing down drywall and hauling debris, tasks I wasn't able to tackle with little ones in tow. But one thing I knew how to do was save money, and so I had already compiled quite a stockpile of cleaning supplies and personal care items. Hearing that our church was a drop-off point for those much-needed cleaning supplies, I gathered as much as I could, put the kids in the minivan, and made our way over there.

Once we made our contribution, I asked if there was any other way we could help. I'll admit, my query was a little halfhearted. After all, I had my kids with me, so it wasn't like I could start helping pull down drywall. But the volunteer coordinator did take me up on my offer in a suitable way. They desperately needed someone to shuttle supplies to the people who were on "ground zero," as well as take supplies and equipment back and forth between our church's main campus downtown and our suburban campus.

Over the coming days, I strapped my babies into their car seats and drove them back and forth through the passable roads in town. While some may not see this type of volunteer service as life-changing, it was to those we helped. And more important, it gave my young children a front-row seat to see how you should give whatever you can in the moment instead of waiting until it "makes sense."

Whenever I speak to someone after they've experienced great loss, or watch an interview on television about a similar situation, I inevitably hear the same sentiment expressed: don't wait until it's too late to appreciate what you have. Gratitude comes in many forms:

- If you want to be grateful for your early morning wake-up call, ask the homeless woman who was laid off six months ago and had to file bankruptcy what that's like.
- If you want to be grateful to be able to swim laps, ask Amy Van Dyken-Rouen, a six-time Olympic gold-medal-winning swimmer who severed her spine in an ATV accident, leaving her paralyzed from the waist down, what that's like.

- If you want your kids to be grateful with just crayons and paper, ask Jennifer Rothschild, who dreamed of becoming an artist but lost most of her sight at fifteen due to a rare form of retinitis pigmentosa, what that's like.
- If your kids are wondering how to express gratitude over bumps and bruises, share the story of Ashlyn Blocker, a teenager who suffers from a rare genetic disorder that prevents her from feeling pain.

Much like joy, gratitude is an expression of a chosen emotion. While we may not like every circumstance we find ourselves in, we can always thank the "one God and Father of all, who is over all and through all and in all" as he goes with us (Eph. 4:6). Our human nature often tricks us into focusing on what we don't have instead of giving thanks for what we do have. As we practice gratitude daily as a family through our words and deeds, we open up a world for our children that may not revolve around them but most certainly can be shaped by them.

! Make It Practical

If nothing else, I want to encourage you to continue carrying on random acts of kindness like we discussed at the end of chapter eight, but now truly implement what it means to be a neighbor: helping to meet the needs of anyone in close proximity to you.

Your city might not have experienced the devastation of a natural disaster like the flood I described earlier, but here are some simple ways you can help your hometown:

- *Drive-by prayer*: Go out into your hometown and explore new neighborhoods, praying over them as you drive by.
- *Drive-through pay it forward*: The next time you find yourself in a drive-through, offer to pay for the order given by the

person in the car behind you. My husband used to work for Starbucks and witnessed such instances on a regular basis, often resulting in more than ten cars following suit, all because one person kicked off the generosity.

- *Family volunteer opportunities*: Ask your church or community center for family-friendly volunteer opportunities already in place.

- *Children's hospital visits*: Call your local children's hospital and see if you and your child can play with, read to, or sit with some of the kids with long-term illnesses. They often get a lot of offers during the holidays, but it's in those in-between times when they can really use volunteers, especially consistent ones.

- *Nursing home visits*: If you were in choir in school, you most likely visited nursing homes over the holidays to sing Christmas carols. But just like the children's hospitals, the residents enjoy visitors throughout the year, not just on major holidays. Call a local nursing home and see if it's possible to take your family to visit. Of course, if you deliver handmade art, create a craft, or even play cards while there, even better.

- *Charity walk*: Enroll your family in a charity walk in your city. Not only will you get to help a cause through your time and fund-raising, but you'll often discover new pockets of your city while on the walk.

- *Highway or street adoption*: Collaborate with other neighbors to adopt a highway or stretch of street in your city that you can be responsible to keep clean on a regular basis.

- *Serve.gov*: Check out this site to find local volunteer opportunities. Or better yet, create your own!

For more practical tips and guidelines, visit SamiCone.com/UncommonKids.

10

PEACE

Option Z

Do you ever put God in a box?

I recently got smacked in the face with my own answer to that question.

As a family, we're always up for trying something new. This typically falls in the realm of experiences or travel, but isn't limited to that. We try to keep our kids open to trying new foods and making new friends, and even trying alternative methods of schooling.

As parents, we put such extreme pressure on ourselves when it comes to deciding what to do when it comes to school choice. My husband and I come from quite different school backgrounds: he grew up going to private Christian school (for the most part), while I grew up in the Chicago public school system (and proud of it). So when it came to deciding how to educate our children, there was no easy or immediately apparent answer.

At the end of our daughter's third-grade year, we felt a shift coming: while we were content with the present situation for Britton, we believed God was calling us to something different for Kariss the pending school year.

Initially, this caused a lot of stress and anxiety. Of course, as a mom, I wanted all the answers right away. We were already dealing with another stressful situation in our family, and I felt like I couldn't handle one more variable. Not only were we trying to do what was best for our children, but we also had to take into consideration the financial burden and inconvenience of what it would mean if they were educated in two different locations.

Because both Kariss and Britton were in private school at the time and school policy called for current families to recommit in the winter semester, we had to arrive at a final decision way before the school year was over. I continued to fret until God gave me an answer (sort of) in my spirit that finally brought peace for the moment: "You don't have to know where Kariss is going to school next fall; you just need to know that it isn't here."

Of course! It was so obvious. Why hadn't I seen it before?

The immediate question in front of me was whether Kariss was going to stay at her current school, not what we were going to do for her schooling the next school year. And because we felt extreme comfort and peace that she was not supposed to stay in the current situation, our first decision was relatively easy.

It was in that moment I remembered the advice a mentor had given me years earlier, before my own children were even in school.

Although she was the daughter of a high school principal, over the course of her children's schooling they experienced homeschool, public, and private school. When I asked her how she came to each decision, she told me that each year was a new opportunity: "When you make a decision about school, take it one year at a time and understand it doesn't mean it will stay that way forever."

It took a great deal of pressure off to know that—much like most things, if we really think about it—a decision is just that, a decision. You make it, you act on it, and if it doesn't work, you make a new one.

When we found peace in the decision to ultimately keep our daughter home at the beginning of fourth grade, God never promised that was where she would stay. It was simply the next step for us in obedience. To be honest, the redirection reminded me of the first verse I embraced as a new Christian who had previously been prone to worry: "Therefore do not worry about tomorrow, for tomorrow will worry about itself. Each day has enough trouble of its own" (Matt. 6:34).

Peace Is a Choice

God intends for each of us to live in peace, just perhaps not the way you or your kids may have previously envisioned.

As we continue in Colossians 3, verse 15 speaks to this specifically: "Let the peace of Christ rule in your hearts, since as members of one body you were called to peace."

Life is ultimately full of choices, and even when we make mistakes, if we seek God's wisdom and guidance, he will always guide us back to his ultimate path for our lives.

"All you need to remember is that God will never let you down; he'll never let you be pushed past your limit; he'll always be there to help you come through it" (1 Cor. 10:13 MSG). This verse reminds us that God always provides a way out for us—an escape clause, if you will. The important aspect to note about this promise is the difference between God's providing a solution for us versus a way for us to remove ourselves from a sticky situation.

Some of us have children who believe not only that they need to understand why everything happens, but that they have the answer for everything. And trying to convince them otherwise can be nearly impossible.

It's in these moments that parents of uncommon kids grasp the opportunity to communicate that we may not always understand the "why" behind the "what," but it's okay because God always does.

Perhaps equally crucial to communicating to our children who God is, is to communicate who we as parents are not.

Peace Doesn't Equal . . .

Being a great parent doesn't require having all the answers. Nor does it mean shielding our children from every twist and turn life may throw at us. On the contrary, our children are guaranteed to have conflict and turmoil. If we then lead them through life believing peace equals the absence of struggles, we are only doing them a disservice.

What our children must see us demonstrate is how we tackle the challenging moments of life and still find peace in the midst of the uncertainty.

In *My Utmost for His Highest*, Oswald Chambers actually suggests that "before we choose to follow God's will, a crisis must develop in our lives. . . . He providentially produces a crisis where we have to decide—for or against. That moment becomes a great crossroads in our lives."[1]

So in essence, we not only need to prepare our children for *if* struggles happen in our lives, but *when* they do. With that preparation comes the practice of peace. If in fact our faith develops out of the crises and critical moments in our lives, our children need to feel confident in the peace that lives within them, and that doesn't come from leading them down a path of ignorance and bliss.

Parenting Mirror: Fresh New Vision

Just as I purposefully breezed over my own emotions when it came to our daughter's fourth-grade school choice, I also left you a bit in the dark about what emotions transpired between us once the experience—an online public school which we simply referred to as "homeschooling"—started to go south.

The programming and curriculum change that occurred after fall break for this particular online school required students to sit in front of the computer many more hours to participate in classes. This was a huge shift from the original structure of the school, and let's just say it did not go over well in our family.

Tears would flow more than once a day, and when Kariss finally burst into an "I hate homeschool" stomp, I knew something had to be done.

Initially I became defensive and hard-hearted over her attitude. We have always shared the motto with our children that "Cones aren't quitters," and we repeatedly remind them they cannot always have what they want when they want it.

You could say I insisted that she change her attitude and exhibit peace.

Funny thing was, in the exact moment of my righteousness, I realized I was not modeling the very attitude I was insisting my daughter adopt.

That same morning, we had just read a story together about Holocaust survivor Corrie ten Boom that ultimately reminded us how every twenty-four hours, God has a fresh, new supply of grace, favor, wisdom, and forgiveness. In her own words:

> Worry does not empty tomorrow of its sorrow; it empties today of its strength. . . . If you look at the world, you'll be distressed. If you look within, you'll be depressed. If you look at God you'll be at rest. . . . Even when it storms, there can still be peace.[2]

Romans 5:3–5 (NLT) echoes these very thoughts of hope and peace:

We can rejoice, too, when we run into problems and trials, for we know that they help us develop endurance. And endurance develops strength of character, and character strengthens our confident hope of salvation. And this hope will not lead to disappointment. For we know how dearly God loves us, because he has given us the Holy Spirit to fill our hearts with his love.

While life may not turn out exactly as we imagine day to day, dwelling in the disappointment only robs us of the hope God has planned for our future. If I could sum up some of the wisdom shared in the previous chapters, adding on a new nugget from this one, I'd say to suck it up, shake it off, and seek his way.

I had gotten the first part right in asking Kariss to shake off the disappointment, but had failed to cast a new vision for where the train would take her.

I removed myself from the volatile situation, both to give her some personal space, which I knew she needed and deserved, and to walk away from the seemingly hopeless situation to seek some clarity.

As I walked downstairs, God revealed to me—as he has done so many times in the past—that I was asking him to choose between options A and B, instead of allowing him to plant option Z in my head.

Aren't we funny like that?

We hold out our two hands, weighing the options before God, thinking he will drop a magical feather onto the choice that is best for us. And even though I have seen it happen so many times in my past, I forget that he may have an even better, more wonderful option in mind for me if I would only allow the space in my heart to receive it.

By the time I got downstairs, I realized something important: we are not bound to any one set standard other than God's. We could adapt our current situation so that our daughter still progressed through her milestones and assessments, while learning about them in different ways.

Every day life will throw us lemons, but it's up to us to choose whether to subject ourselves to the sour fruit in front of us or to enlist some sugar to sweeten the deal. Even in the most dire situations, we can find contentment when we rest in knowing our peace ultimately comes from heaven above.

Walking Out Your Faith

Our school choice dilemma ultimately taught us that peace comes from walking out your faith.

Even if we want to, we can't stay put in our current circumstances. Kids have to go to school, parents have to go to work, and life goes on. While we didn't let our daughter quit a difficult situation in the midst of it, we did encourage her to start to explore new options. We researched other programs and even visited new schools that she could begin the next semester.

Peace doesn't come from the change itself; it comes from moving in the direction you're called to.

But one thing we didn't tolerate was self-pity or bitterness. If she wanted to change her predicament, she needed to start by being the change she wanted to see.

Eleanor Roosevelt said, "Peace will not be built, however, by people with bitterness in their hearts. . . . For it isn't enough to talk of peace. One must believe it. And it isn't enough to believe in it. One must work at it."[3]

If you have a belief, you need to walk through it. Peace doesn't come from the change itself; it comes from moving in the direction you're called to.

Ultimately, what Kariss needed ended up being right in front of our eyes—literally. For the second semester of her fourth-grade year, she began attending the public elementary school less than a mile from our home. At the beginning of the next school year, Britton ended up joining her there.

MENTOR MOMENT
FINDING PEACE IN THE LETTING GO

When it comes to demystifying mom life, there's one mom in particular I think about. Since I have yet to experience what it's like to have children move away from our home, I asked Tracey Eyster if she'd be willing to share her experience. What she says here is a testimony of not only her peace but also the peace it allowed her son to experience because she knew that she was at ease with where God had her in those moments.

The first time I really heard my son's declaration of independence from mom rule was as a tween. We were about to go on a family trip and I was drilling him on—I mean, "helping" him determine what he needed to pack. As I was spouting out orders, he stood upright, looked me in the eye, and with a gentle but determined voice said, "I got this." This mom general's initial reaction was to overrule his assumption that he was equipped to pack his own suitcase and fire out a barrage of orders. Thankfully the soft nudge of the Holy Spirit silenced the rapid succession of words straining to be released.

A new enlightenment began to swirl through my mom brain that day: *If you want him to be ready to march out of here successfully someday and be a strong and courageous man, you have to start letting go, bit by bit, day by day.* Yes, it is hard, mamas—but we must.

The only way my son could become a warrior for God was if I allowed him small daily victories of independence from me, and dependence on God, while growing and maturing in our home. He and I never formed a battle plan of how I was to "let go," but it was interesting that those three words became his way of revealing my encroachment and his need for growth. He became very aware of my intentional backing off when he uttered those revealing words,

Some may criticize us for the amount of change we're exposing our children to. I believe we're simply walking them through the life the world has for them, but under the safety of our roof so we can process every part of it with them.

Uncommon kids are not those who have been removed from

"I got this." The benefit? I noticed that with each encounter his head lifted higher, his chest puffed out a bit more, and the man in him grew in confidence. He lived up to the expectation that he did indeed have what it takes.

In this process of backing off, I was given profound peace in knowing that my son was stepping into his future while under the watchful care and loving guidance of his father and me. Giving him space to succeed (and fail) while still at home was growing confidence, in all of us, for his future.

Just last year my son made the decision to go to a technical college in Orlando, Florida; it's nearly a thousand miles from home. After a few months of getting used to his surroundings, serving at a church, and building godly relationships, he is thriving and continues to grow into the capable, courageous man God has designed him to be.

Many have commented on how hard it must be that he is so far away and on his own, rather than living in dorms or with someone we know. And yes, I have regularly prayed Philippians 4:4–9 over both him and me, but peace reigns in this mom heart and in his. He has faced every challenge with steadfast determination and complete trust in God.

I am beyond grateful that a peace that transcends all understanding has settled on me since my son drove away several months ago. At every point in the launching process, if I have shown signs of a need to over engage and protect, my son has looked me in the eye, smiled softly, and reminded me, "I got this."[4]

Tracey Eyster is a wife, a mom of two, the founder/creator of MomLifeToday.com and MomLife Boot Camp, author of Be the Mom and LifeWay's Beautiful Mess Bible study, and co-host of the Encouragement Café radio show and podcast the world but rather those who have been exposed to the world but choose God's kingdom instead.

Release Control, Not Responsibility

God calls us to release control, not responsibility.

You've likely heard the term "helicopter parent" in the media. This modern-day concept refers to a parent who constantly hovers around his or her children, barely letting them move or breathe on their own.

Yet the Bible clearly states our role as parents is not to manipulate our children into doing what's right but to model what is expected so they can ultimately take responsibility for their own actions.

Zig Ziglar famously warned us, "If you aim at nothing, you will hit it every time." If we never set an expectation for our children, we have no one to blame but ourselves when they don't meet it.

> *God calls us to release control, not responsibility.*

I'll bet for most of you reading this right now, spankings were not uncommon when you were growing up. In fact, I'll go a step further and bet that most adults today have, at one time or another, experienced "disciplining" with a belt, paddle, or switch.

While I would never condone physical abuse of a child, I'm afraid we've gone too far in the other direction as parents, steering clear from any form of discipline whatsoever.

Hebrews 12:11 reminds us that "no discipline seems pleasant at the time, but painful. Later on, however, it produces a harvest of righteousness and peace for those who have been trained by it."

In this verse, "peace" has little to do with circumstance and everything to do with a state of being. In fact, it denotes "a state of untroubled, undisturbed well-being."[5]

Instead of being so concerned with being our kids' friends, we need to step up as parents to remind them that whether or not they like us in any given moment, they can be confident in knowing they are loved.

Peace in Action

Once our children truly believe they are loved unconditionally by us as their parents, they begin to trust us in a new way. Out of that trust, kids begin to spread their wings and make an impact around them.

For the next generation to change what others think, they first need to be firmly cemented in their own beliefs. And while knowing the truth is important, they also need to remain perpetual learners.

Once our children truly believe they are loved unconditionally by us as their parents, they begin to trust us in a new way.

Ephesians 4:1 and 13 remind us that, as Christians, we are urged "to live a life worthy of the calling you have received . . . until we all reach unity in the faith and in the knowledge of the Son of God and become mature, attaining to the whole measure of the fullness of Christ."

When this happens, verse 14 says, "Then we will no longer be infants, tossed back and forth by the waves, and blown here and there by every wind of teaching and by the cunning and craftiness of people in their deceitful scheming." While our faith may be absolute, each individual's path to discovering it varies. That being said, understanding just how to share our faith can be cause for trepidation, especially with our children.

While not a child when I came to truly know Christ in my midtwenties, I embodied this sense of childlike faith. Although I was on fire for the Lord and wanted to share this newfound love and knowledge with everyone I met, I more often than not let fear stand in my way: I came to falsely believe that others' salvation hinged on how eloquently I could present the gospel message to them.

So instead of sharing my unbridled passion for my Savior, who'd set me free from my people-pleasing tendencies, I once again found myself caught up in worrying that I wasn't enough.

But at least I was in good company: Moses, Esther, and even Noah at one time doubted whether God could use them to fulfill his purposes. Thankfully, all of us served a God who knows better.

Yet I distinctly remember one instance shortly after I'd committed my life to Christ when I longed for God to tangibly show me how to share my faith. Returning from a business conference, I was sitting in an airport with my study Bible in my lap, internally debating with God. A young couple arrived and sat directly across from me, choosing to sit next to a man in a wheelchair whom I'd neglected to acknowledge because, ironically, I was too busy worrying about how I could serve God.

Before I knew it, this delightful couple had started a casual conversation with the gentleman. What began with mundane pleasantries about travel plans evolved into talk of family and hardships. Within minutes, they asked if they could pray with him, and he hesitantly yet gratefully accepted their offer.

As soon as the prayer ended, the couple realized they'd been at the wrong gate all along. They quickly excused themselves, exchanging one more set of pleasantries with their new friend, and then started to walk away.

I sat and stared in amazement. There was no preaching, no flipping through a Bible to find the right verse, and certainly no altar call. Instead, I simply saw two people take an interest in someone else. They shared their story and, more important, they listened to his.

Before the couple could get very far, I shook myself out of my stupor and called after them. I confessed how just minutes prior to their arrival I'd prayed for God to show me how to share my faith, and told them their "accidental" arrival was no accident. They smiled and gently encouraged me before they continued on to their intended destination.

Sometimes people misconstrue peace as passivity. To the contrary, we are to "seek peace and pursue it" (Ps. 34:14). If we are to "make every effort to live in peace with everyone and to be holy" (Heb. 12:14), we can't always wait for the opportunity to appear in front of us. We must lead our children in the charge toward it.

The Call of Peace

Peace is strong. Peace is mighty. And most important, peace is the object of divine promise brought about by God's mercy. Just as peace represents the reconciled relationship between God and man, so must we strive to perpetuate that peace among our fellow human beings.

Philosophy professor and author Dallas Willard defined peace as "the deep rest and assurance of good that comes from complete abandonment to God."[6] Notice there is no mention of assurance that everything will turn out the way we want, or even that everything will turn out hunky-dory. There is, however, one sure way to receive the peace of God, and Philippians 4:6–7 describes how:

> Do not be anxious about anything, but in every situation, by prayer and petition, with thanksgiving, present your requests to God. And the peace of God, which transcends all understanding, will guard your hearts and your minds in Christ Jesus.

When your children come to embrace this understanding of peace, not only will they be able to go out of your home with the comfort of God's covering over their lives, but you too will rest in the peace it provides as a parent.

❗ Make It Practical

When we examine putting peace into practice, it can be accomplished simply through sharing your faith, like in the example above, or it can take on a more literal approach, such as in playing a more active role in the governing laws of your state.

As a family, you and your kids can still get involved on state-level decisions that directly affect you, and it doesn't have to be anything as major as same-sex marriage laws or as mundane as zoning rights. Though the ideas below may not be implemented as much among families, that's all the more reason why your voice and beliefs need to be heard. Plus, just think of the impact it will make on your children to know they've influenced the state in which they live. Here are a few suggestions:

- *Learn the laws*: To make a difference in your state, you first need to know individual state laws. Talk with your family about what they would specifically change if they could in your state and then research the laws surrounding the issue. The education alone is a great step in becoming a better citizen, but make every effort to follow through with action as well.

- *Write your state representatives*: Speaking of taking action, write to your state representatives on behalf of the cause you researched above. In my experience, writing a physical letter is the best way to make the experience resonate with your children, but you could also consider an email or phone call.

- *Start a petition*: To come full circle with the options above, start a petition. Once you've researched a law and contacted your state representative about it, rally others to help implement that change. With the internet being what it is today, it's even easier to garner support.

- *Volunteer at competitions*: You name it, there's a competition for it. State competitions exist for sports, academics, arts, and more, and by volunteering, not only do you get to attend for free, your kids are more likely to be inspired to take their interests to the next level. So choose something you're passionate about and you just might make some new friends who love what you do as well!

- *Meet a need*: Find a fun way to meet a need. When you expand your volunteer focus outside of just your city, you'd be amazed at the opportunities that open up for your family. Broadening the circle, so to speak, allows you to get involved with an organization that aligns with your family's particular interests or even just take a more creative approach to volunteering. Organizations like Swing Higher, which "partners with God and people to build and support community play spaces for underserved children," always needs volunteers and would be a great fund-raising beneficiary.

For more practical tips and guidelines, visit SamiCone.com/UncommonKids.

11

HUMILITY

Consider Others

Something may be good for somebody, but not everything is good for everybody.

Whenever I find clothing or a hat with a label that reads "one size fits all," I chuckle to myself. Isn't that phrase, by nature, an oxymoron?

It's almost like they're not even pretending to tell us the truth. How could one hat fit every human being on the planet? It would be better if they say one size fits some or no size fits all.

The same principle applies to our children and our parenting.

Wouldn't it be nice if we could say the same thing to every child and they all responded exactly the same way? By the simple fact that you are reading this book, I can tell you already know how preposterous that statement is.

After all, it's hard enough to get my husband to understand me, let alone both of my children.

Different Children, Different Needs

When our oldest child was still a toddler, we discovered an important method for how to speak to her in conflict.

While we believe, and continue to believe, that issues must be dealt with head-on as soon as possible, when we spoke with her face-to-face, she was more concerned about being right and getting to talk than she was with listening to us. Getting on her level and being eye to eye made her more defensive instead of helping her engage.

One day after a disagreement before bed, I used two of her stuffed animals to reenact the scene we had just experienced. No longer was she an active participant in the confrontation but a third-party spectator who could see the incident from a higher level and process it more thoughtfully.

Instead of feeling attacked, Kariss felt like a counselor whose advice I was seeking. By talking about the events in third person and allowing her a little more time to see her role in what happened, she came to understand what was best much more quickly than when we confronted her directly.

We continue to use this technique to this day, sometimes with props and sometimes just by sitting back-to-back instead of face-to-face.

If we ever tried this technique with our youngest, I don't think it would have near the same effect. Britton is a different personality than our daughter, and instead of pulling away from conflict like she does, he tends to crawl into our laps and get very close, even when we are angry with him.

As you can see, the one-size-fits-all theory does not apply to our family, much like I imagine it cannot apply to yours.

As I've tried to stress throughout this book, the key is to model how we hope our children will treat others.

You Can't Win

In his timeless bestseller *How to Win Friends and Influence People*, Dale Carnegie espouses "the only way to get the best of an argument is to avoid it." He explains further:

> You can't win an argument. You can't because if you lose it, you lose it; and if you win it, you lose it. Why? Well, suppose you triumph over the other man and show his argument full of holes and prove that he is *non compos mentis*. Then what? You will feel fine. But what about him? You have made him feel inferior. You have hurt his pride. He will resent your triumph.[1]

Regardless of the age of our children, it seems like they know how to fight for their rights. Being that we are all born as selfish beings, it seems natural to fight for what we want. All arguments come down to the fact that we believe we are right while simultaneously believing that someone else is wrong.

Andy Stanley teaches that if we all made one simple realization at the beginning of each argument, it would diffuse the majority of heartache we face: the problem we ultimately have with other people is that they don't behave the way we expect them to. We need to step back and focus more on changing ourselves and our attitude instead of focusing on the behavior of others, over which we have no control.

We must consider others more than ourselves.

We must put away pride.

We must embrace humility.

Philippians 2:3 sums this concept up perfectly: "Do nothing out of selfish ambition or vain conceit. Rather, in humility value others above yourselves."

We quickly learned that instead of trying to win arguments with our kids, we needed to understand how we each react in heated situations and then work together to communicate as effectively as possible. Now in doing so, regardless of how each member of our family handles conflict, our values stay the same in all situations.

Our children know that any of the "3 Ds"—disrespect, dishonesty, disobedience—result in consequences. Those consequences may look different during the various ages and stages of their growing-up years, but make no mistake, there will be consequences.

In much the same way, each child receives rewards once they reach a certain level of trust, responsibility, and maturity. We would be foolish to think accomplishment in these areas automatically happens at the same age with each of our children.

This principle applies in our children's peer relationships too; they cannot expect to behave the same way with each of their friends and get the same results. They can, however, maintain their core values regardless of who they are around and what situations they find themselves in.

The beautiful lesson this teaches our children is that, although everyone cannot help everybody, someone can help somebody. This simple concept demystifies the definition of serving others.

We don't have to have any special skills, talents, or agenda. We only need to teach our children to tap into what it is they love and find others who are interested in sharing the same gifts.

Parenting Mirror: Are You Interesting?

Let's face it. We're all good at some things and not at others. But if we continue on the theme "someone can help somebody," then we could also say everyone has something to give. The key lies in helping our children discover their individual gifts and talents.

Let me pause here to give one caveat.

When we become parents, we gain a new life in our family. But too often, we also allow a piece of ourselves to die. We mistakenly believe that to give our kids everything, we have to give up what we love.

The reality is that to help our kids discover their own talents, we must first self-assess what we have to offer as individuals. As important as it is for our kids to know we love them, they also have to understand that our lives don't revolve around them.

They can't.

To make our children the center of our world actually does them a disservice. Not only does it create the exact opposite of humility in them; it prevents them from getting to know who we are as individuals outside of being their parents.

Think back to when you and your mate first met. What attracted him or her to you the most? Now think back to before you had kids. What would you choose to do if you had a free Friday night or Saturday? Where would you go?

Now come back to the present. When was the last time you set personal goals? When was the last time you tried something new?

Better yet, if I interviewed your kids, what would they say you love to do? If their answer is "cleaning" or "looking at an iPhone," then you have a problem.

Instead, consider what you want to be known for. Obviously we all want to be known for our love for God and our family, but what are your passions beyond that? What inspires you? What makes you unique and interesting? In discovering these things about yourself, you'll be able to better help your kids to do the same.

Discover Their Gifts

Helping your children discover their God-given gifts doesn't have to be difficult.

While there are a number of tools out there to help you on this journey, there is a simple technique I recommend you start with: listen and observe.

Let's face it, you have a lot on your plate as it is, so don't make this any harder than it needs to be. Just take the time to listen to your children and observe what it is they like to do.

Remember those questions I made you ask of yourself a few paragraphs ago? Now I want you to consider them in light of your children. What are they passionate about? What inspires them? What makes them unique and interesting?

Now go a step beyond those initial questions: What would they choose to do if you gave them free rein for a weekend? If they could travel anywhere, where would it be? What is their favorite subject in school? Do they participate in any extracurricular activities? Who are their best friends and what do they do when they're together?

While the answers will not provide definitive direction when it comes to discovering your children's gifts and talents, they will help you to discern not only how they can help others but also where they want to lend their time and talents.

Even if you think you know the answers to these questions about your children, make time to schedule a one-on-one date with each of them. As our children grow, their tastes and interests change, so what may have been true even a year ago may not be true now.

Making the effort to spend time with your kids on their conditions at a place of their choosing will not only give you a special glimpse into their minds, hearts, and lives, but afford them the opportunity to get to know a different side of you as well.

No matter what, don't let this process get in the way of getting out there and helping someone in need. Sometimes we don't discover our true calling until we experience an event that challenges our comfort level.

Helping in Haiti

This takes me back to a mission trip I took to Haiti before I got married. When we went out into the field, we were told to simply love on the kids. We weren't told whether we should color, paint nails, play soccer, or braid hair. Our instructions were to love.

Within thirty seconds of being in the midst of a gaggle of kids, it became obvious what each preferred to do and how we could demonstrate love to them. We quickly found a pickup game of soccer with a ball made out of numerous plastic grocery bags tied together; a game of ring-around-the-rosy in another corner; an intense game of keep-away somewhere else; and a group of girls piling on a group of us so they could "do" our hair, marveling at its fine texture.

If our group leader had tried to corral us, divide us into teams, instruct us in different games, and assign us a certain number of children, it most likely would have backfired miserably. Instead, we were given freedom. A wise person once said, "Preach the gospel and when necessary use words." It's true. It didn't matter that hardly anyone could understand each other in this setting; the kids felt the love.

Different Expectations

This memory makes me think about my children's definition of a good babysitter. We have not left our children with a lot of babysitters, and when we do we are quite particular about whose company we leave them in. So it always surprises me to hear that they like some babysitters and not others.

One day Kariss confided that she didn't have as much fun with one of her babysitters as she thought she was going to. After all, she knew this person well and had even been excited about spending time with her.

But when I pressed my daughter, I discovered her criteria for a good babysitter was quite simple: whether or not they played with her and her brother while we were gone. She didn't care about

references, past experience, cooking abilities, or safety certifica-
tions. All she wanted was to be played with and given undivided
attention.

Just as Kariss and I had different expectations when it came to finding a "good" babysitter, so too do parents and children often have different expectations when it comes to humility and serving others. It further proves an important point: expectations cannot be assumed; they must be communicated.

> *Expectations cannot be assumed; they must be communicated.*

When it comes to our kids, we can assume nothing. (Anyone who's ever taken a toddler on a grocery store excursion can testify to this fact.) While surely you may think your kids will be sensitive and defer to those less fortunate than them, believe me, without proper communication this isn't always the case.

As I mentioned earlier, the major problem facing today's youth is that they've been told (or at least made to believe) that the world revolves around them. This creates a prideful foundation in our kids, making them unaware of the needs of other people. With such insensitivity, they can't be expected to reach out and help those around them.

Third World Problems, First World Location

It's hard to believe so many people in America are living below the poverty level. With the multitude of resources we have at our disposal, how can a large percentage of Americans be lacking even the most basic needs?

In chapter seven I talked about my attitude toward the first mission trip our family took to a small town in Kentucky in partnership with our church, but I didn't share much about the transformation my daughter experienced while there.

Not long into the eight-hour drive, our kids started complaining as if we were just on a regular road trip vacation: they didn't like the movie on our van's DVD player, they wanted to stop to eat, and, as on any road trip, they continually asked, "How much longer?" It quickly became clear that our children had no concept of what this trip was going to be like or who we were going to come in contact with. We feebly attempted to redirect their thinking on the remainder of the trip, but nothing could have prepared them like actually arriving at the town's community center.

As our church group pulled in during the dark hours of a Friday evening, we found a dilapidated and seemingly deserted gymnasium with broken windows and no air-conditioning. If it hadn't sunk in already, my husband and I became acutely aware that this trip had nothing to do with our own comfort level. Yet this still didn't sink in for our kids.

The bickering continued over everything from who would get the bigger blow-up mattress to the lack of breakfast options the following morning. As we readied ourselves for the back-to-school bash, barbecue, and school supply giveaways in a park, Kariss especially still seemed to try to fit this unknown land into her world instead of the other way around.

In essence, she expected the spotlight on her when instead, to be effective, she had to fade into the background.

It wasn't until the neighborhood kids started arriving at our event and she saw me take the lead as a face painter that something started to click.

"But, Mommy, you don't know how to paint!"

I told her, "It's not about knowing how to do something. It's about being willing to do anything."

In the meantime, her little brother had already made quick friends by introducing some sort of a ball into the mix. As Kariss took a step back from my rapidly growing line of face-painting fans, she finally seemed to grasp that we weren't there to cater to her needs. She found a girl similar in age and asked if she wanted to play.

That afternoon, amid sweltering temperatures, major cultural divides, and water balloon fights, we all found our own way. After a couple of hours fine-tuning my facial-art skills, I took a break to eat an overly charred cheeseburger and just take a step back to observe.

> *It's not about knowing how to do something. It's about being willing to do anything.*

While my natural tendency is to act like a helicopter mom and hover as I cautioned you all not to do earlier, I found myself standing in the shadows, literally. Although we typically enjoy doing things together as a family, it was sweet to watch each of my family members scattered throughout the park, all doing something different yet equally impactful.

It wasn't until our kids experienced this type of service firsthand that they were finally able to make sense of 1 Peter 5:6: "Humble yourselves, therefore, under God's mighty hand, that he may lift you up in due time."

Once we put the needs of others before our own, then we will truly understand the meaning of humility. And it wasn't until our children traveled outside of their comfort zone that they truly understood how much their impact on others depended not on their talents but on their willingness to serve.

Outside of Yourself

An essential component of humility is gratitude.

When my children spent the first leg of our Kentucky mission trip focused only on themselves, their feelings, and their abilities, the task at hand seemed impossible to them at most and at least undesirable.

When they instead put themselves aside and made room for the Spirit of God to work in and through them, beautiful things happened. Colossians 3:17 finally began to come alive within them: "And whatever you do, whether in word or deed, do it all in the name of the Lord Jesus, giving thanks to God the Father through him."

I couldn't make this happen, but . . .

I could encourage them.

I could coax them.

I could lead them.

Ultimately, they had to experience the transformation themselves.

For both of my children, and for our family as a whole, this meant stepping outside of our comfort zones. And I don't mean only in the physical sense.

Several moments during our family mission trip came up as incompatible with our typical frame of reference. One instance in particular was when Kariss saw a child playing on an iPad. She immediately challenged me: "I thought you said they were poor, Mom."

I had no ready answer for her, and I noticed her need for justice begin to swell within her. As I frantically searched for an explanation in my own head, I felt God quiet my attempt. Our ministry was not to come and judge what these people were doing or how they were doing it; our responsibility was only to serve and love.

To Agree or Disagree

Showing love does not require that we agree, even when it comes to politics and religion.

I often liken my take on politics to my own faith walk. When people ask about my religion, more often than not they're not satisfied when I tell them, "I'm a Christian."

"Yes, but what denomination are you?"

"I believe in the Bible and I love Jesus."

Perhaps it's from not growing up in the church, but I've never understood the reason for division within a particular faith. It's

MENTOR MOMENT
PRACTICING WHAT YOU BELIEVE

There comes a point for all parents when they have to let go and trust that their kids have absorbed the lessons they've modeled for them. But that can be easier said than done when your kids are on a national stage, literally. When it came to finding wise words on humility, I sought out my friend Reese Dixon. Watching her talented children (Colton Dixon and Schyler Dixon) perform before a television audience of millions on *American Idol* could have been scary for multiple reasons, but it allowed her and her husband, Mike, to experience the joy that comes from raising uncommon kids.

I believe that, as a parent, I have a tremendous responsibility to raise my children, impacting them in every way. From that first year, we spent every day praying, teaching, loving, and showing our children how to practice what you preach. We were not perfect and made many mistakes, but we held ourselves accountable as we did our children, teaching them with biblical principles while applying them in our daily lives. In doing this and by actively supporting them, we have had an amazing life with countless memories from playing every sport to their pursuit of a music career.

These principles and values have seen practical application as they have begun this journey in music. Both our children auditioned for *American Idol*. And so began the two-year journey that would be Colton and Schyler's growth, not only as brother and sister, but as young Christians in a not-so-Christian environment.

Both did well that first year but did not make it into the final rounds. Sky went back for her second audition year and made it to the judges' round, where the judges and producers asked Colton to come in with her and also audition unexpectedly. Both once again made the cut.

a feeling that's carried over to my politics. When others question my political party affiliation, I respond, "I'm American."

After all, how could I agree or disagree with someone based solely on what side of the aisle they sit on? It's just as asinine to

The coming weeks and months were very hard on our family. The show is a platform for talented kids to be seen and promoted, but the environment can be a very lonely, stressful place for kids trying to find their way in life and career. It can also cause internal issues within a family as these kids are getting pushed and pulled and put in situations where they must make decisions that could be counter to their faith and who they are. We discussed that no matter how far they made it on the show, their character and who they truly are was the most important thing.

We reminded them of 1 Timothy 1:19: "Holding on to faith and a good conscience, which some have rejected and so have suffered shipwreck with regard to the faith." Both kids made it to the top 40, then both were eliminated.

The brother-sister love they have for one another is amazing. Everyone has choices, from temptation, fame, and pride to how they react to adversity or accolades, and so on. Practicing what you believe, walking in your faith, and remaining humble can and will impact others. You never know who is watching how you handle things and how that may help them.

In the end, when Colton was voted off, he chose to unexpectedly kneel and thank God for this amazing opportunity and sing with hand raised, praising God as the show ended that night. Never before has the show had such an outward display of faith by a contestant. This is what it is all about: sharing our faith and practicing what we preach without fear of what anyone thinks. I can honestly say that we have truly enjoyed our kids and continue to learn and grow as we experience new adventures and memories each year even though they are now young adults. They make me a proud momma, not because of their talents but because of their character![2]

Teresa ("Reese") Dixon is wife to Mike and mother of two.

say I agree or disagree with someone based solely on their religious denomination.

As parents, we have to ingrain in our children that their sense of humility and serving cannot depend on whether we think the recipient *deserves* our service. If Holocaust survivors can forgive Nazi soldiers who tortured them and former Southern slaves can forgive their former masters, then surely we can humble ourselves enough to not take generational offenses on ourselves or pass them on to our children.

It's not about being right; it's about putting feet to our faith.

Teaching your kids not to be prideful also means teaching them to care about our country as a whole. Even raising their awareness is a step in the right direction.

This can be as simple as informing your children about current events affecting our nation or demonstrating what it means to respect those in political office even when you don't agree with their policies.

After all, what we're experiencing as a nation today isn't that far off from the cultural and political troubles we read about in the Bible. But if we are going to prepare our children to change the state of our nation, we first need to represent what it truly means to submit ourselves to and humble ourselves under the authority of the one true God.

! Make It Practical

Several terms expressing humility in the Bible can be interchanged with meekness, yet the Greek root is not typically expressed in English because in our culture meekness is often associated with weakness. The reality, however, is that meekness represents a condition of the mind and heart that demonstrates gentleness, *not* in weakness but in power. It is a balance born in strength of character.

This strength of character makes it possible for our families to stand up for what we believe in and help others to do the same. Making an impact in our nation does not necessarily mean serving in the armed forces, though many of our children will grow up to aspire to this level of service. These suggestions, however, are ones your family can implement right away:

- *Pray for leadership*: One of the easiest ways to model for your kids how to impact our nation is to pray for our nation's leadership, regardless of whether you agree with them or their policies.

- *Celebrate "annual days"*: Find a way to celebrate different "annual days," such as See You at the Pole or Earth Day, either as a family or as a group within your community. Even making a big deal about national family holidays like Grandparents Day allows our kids to put those they love ahead of themselves while brightening someone else's day.

- *Support a national charity*: The ALS Ice Bucket Challenge brought a national cause to life in a way we could all tangibly help. Encourage your kids to contact a national cause and ask how they can help at a local level.

- *Write to members of the military*: It's hard for anyone to imagine what it's like to serve our country in the military unless they have experienced it firsthand. But it's not hard to imagine what it's like to be thousands of miles away from your family. Many organizations give guidance in writing and sending care packages to the active duty members of our military.

For more practical tips and guidelines, visit SamiCone.com/UncommonKids.

12

COMPASSION

Both/And

We've finally reached the place where many of you probably hoped I would have started. (In fact, some of you may have skipped ahead to read this chapter first!)

While raising uncommon kids does not necessarily follow a sequential rationale, following the foundational steps—starting small and personal and building to love for humanity in general—certainly makes the path more clear.

I've always found comfort in 2 Peter 1:5–7:

> Make every effort to add to your faith goodness; and to goodness, knowledge; and to knowledge, self-control; and to self-control, perseverance; and to perseverance, godliness; and to godliness, mutual affection; and to mutual affection, love.

But it's verse 8 that truly intrigues and encourages me:

> For if you possess these qualities in increasing measure, they will keep you from being ineffective and unproductive in your knowledge of our Lord Jesus Christ.

Second Peter 1:5–7 not only reminds me of the fruit of the Spirit found in Galatians 5:22–23 in content, but both passages embrace another similarity: they build upon each other.

Much like the eleven character traits I've already discussed—love, harmony, gentleness, bearing with, forgiveness, wisdom, patience, kindness, gratitude, peace, and humility—which are based on Colossians 3, the two passages above describe qualities that work best in unison.

In fact, we see a big misconception about the fruit of the Spirit when it is referred to as the fruits of the Spirit. While many characteristics are mentioned in Galatians 5:22–23, they are referred to singularly as the fruit of the Spirit, indicating their dependence upon one another.

To be completely honest, when I first made this discovery, it intimidated me a little. After all, how could I possibly possess all those traits? But then I happened upon 1 Peter 5:8. Did you notice the verbiage? "If you possess these qualities in increasing measure, they will keep you from being *ineffective* and *unproductive* in your knowledge of our Lord Jesus Christ" (emphasis added).

That's right! These qualities will keep us from being ineffective and unproductive. It says nothing about great accomplishments of wisdom and feats of knowledge that are expected of me as a child of God. No! These qualities keep me from being unproductive.

If a parent could ever get behind any prayer, it's this one. In fact, I literally turned this passage of Scripture into a prayer once I became a mom.

As an only child, I had no idea what I was doing when they handed me my first baby in the hospital. I remember the nurse coming into our hospital room two days after my son was born, saying, "Everything looks great, so we're going to try to hurry and get you home!" All I could think of was, "What's the rush?" After all, I had someone bringing me food and medicine whenever I needed it, not to mention nurses who would actually come help me at any hour of the day if I couldn't figure out something about my baby. Who would want to leave that?

So when I say I embraced these verses about preventing me from being ineffective and unproductive, trust me when I tell you they spoke to my heart. Instead of reading those qualities as mandates, I saw them as encouragement for a heart like mine needing that extra push of help.

Likewise, I pray the eleven qualities I've shared thus far will encourage and properly equip you for sharing the twelfth and final characteristic with your children: compassion.

As parents, it's our job to help our kids embrace God's richest blessings *and* have a heart to heal a hurting world. How, what, and when we communicate to our children affects not only our relationships with them but ultimately their worldview.

So how then do we reconcile our children to the fact that while we excite and entice them by throwing elaborate birthday parties and taking grand vacations, we then chastise them for not having the innate desire to go without for the sake of identifying with and helping the orphans and less fortunate?

I would suggest that it doesn't have to be either/or but rather can be both/and.

As the daughter of a first-generation American born during the Great Depression, I lived with a single phrase playing over and over again in my head: "We don't have money for that."

When you are told you don't have enough of something, not only does it leave you feeling perpetually unsatisfied with what you do have; it leaves you always feeling like you need more.

But perhaps the worst side effect is the fear. Not so much a fear of not having, though that exists too, but more of a controlling fear.

Today I go by the moniker "Savings Expert" and "Frugal Mom," yet all my efforts stemmed from a fear of money. Growing up with a single mom, I learned from an early age that if I wanted something, I'd most likely have to win it or save for it. This fear of not having enough money kept me living in a scarcity mentality until recently when it finally sunk in that money is not inherently good or evil. When such connections are not made for our children, they are left to construct their own truths.

MENTOR MOMENT
LOOK AROUND YOU

I couldn't think of a more appropriate mentor to go to for this final mentor moment than my own mother. Not only has she lived in many parts of the world, but as someone who also came to know Christ later in life, her unique perspective on compassion is one we can all learn from.

I was born in England just after WWII. I always knew my father never wanted kids, but my mother loved us and tried to compensate by working so we could have a few more things than rationing would allow. My earliest memories are of walking my younger brother to school, making him "tea" after school, and cleaning the house. My brother adapted by becoming the "good" one, but I rebelled and wanted out ASAP. My chance came when a favorite aunt offered me an airline ticket at age fifteen and I flew to Africa to work as a secretary in Lusaka, Northern Rhodesia. I was amazed at the difference between living in a comfortable bungalow and our "houseboy" and his family sharing one concrete room attached to the garage. I could hear drums at night, coming from the nearby "ghetto" where families lived in squalor while I was sheltered in the European lifestyle. Unable to remain in Africa due to political unrest, I worked for a year in England before escaping to the United States as an au pair to six children, north of Chicago. Fast-forward to the miracle of my daughter's birth (and I do mean *miracle*). I

As we discussed in chapter five, I'm not a believer in disclosing every detail of our troubles to our children, but I do believe our children find security in knowledge.

The true beauty of the Christian life is recognizing just how much God wants to richly bless us. The underlying problem comes, however, when we flaunt wealth, fail to pay it forward, and live with it in perpetual guilt.

So how do we help our kids relate to the less fortunate children of the world? It seems our kids have no concept of how much "stuff" they have. We don't want to make them feel guilty, but

had no learned parenting skills, but I wanted her to have what I didn't—the knowledge that she was loved unconditionally.

As a child and teen, I responded selfishly even after I learned the Lord's path. While I am truly grateful that God pursued me recklessly and never gave up, I wish I had opened my eyes and heart and hands earlier to those in need. As someone who grew up with very little, I strove to give my daughter everything I didn't have, physically and emotionally. My ex-husband and I both agreed on the importance of education and extracurricular activities, so we encouraged our daughter to explore her mental and physical capabilities to the fullest. While she may not have observed the same conditions I did around the world in my youth, I fully supported her decision as a young adult to serve in Haiti, Mexico, and anywhere else where there were children and families in need.

There will always be situations where God's people have the opportunity to step forward and show his loving-kindness, even if we speak different languages. Parents choosing to model God's love and compassion to their children are providing a precious foundation to impact the world around them.[1]

Dawn P. Strauss is the blessed mother of one and proud "Mumsy" to two special grandkids who have challenged her sewing skills to make many different Disney costumes and her building skills to make a "Buzz Lightyear bunk bed" and, most recently, the "Cone Castle."

how on earth can we expect them to understand what it's like to live without a toilet and running water?

Real Parent Dilemma

I completely identify with this scenario. I struggled (and still do) with that same question. In fact, have you ever seen those commercials on television asking for a dollar a day to help a child across the globe? Or perhaps you've threatened your kids to eat their vegetables by saying, "Do you know there are kids starving in Africa because they have no food?" Perhaps you've even thought to yourself, *"It's unfortunate that children are hurting, but there's not really any tangible way I can help."*

I used to be one of those people.

Well no, I take that back. I sponsored a child back when I was in my twenties (and believe me, it's strange to say that as my forties are getting closer and my twenties are getting further behind me). I was a new Christian at the time with a little extra spending money, and sponsoring a child seemed like the "right" thing to do.

So I signed up, put her picture on the fridge, and prayed for her when I went to get my late-night snacks. I didn't get much communication from her and, to be honest, I felt a big disconnect. I knew nothing about her, where she was from, what her family was going through, or what she needed from me. I even started to doubt whether my money was even getting to her.

So I stopped.

After all, at least I had tried, right?

Fast-forward about ten years when the tragic earthquake struck Haiti in 2010. As a French speaker and someone who had previously visited Haiti on a mission trip, this international tragedy struck me especially hard. But it wasn't until my (then) four- and five-year-old children and I attended a benefit concert my husband was helping with that I knew things had to change. After images from the disaster flashed on the screen, I faced for the first time questions like these from my children:

"Mommy, are those real kids?"

"Why are they eating mud?"

"Where are their shoes?"

"What happens to them now that their mommy and daddy are dead?"

"Can they come live with us?"

From that moment on, I knew our lives could not be the same.

I got more practical and prayerful with my kids when it came to helping others. We bought groceries for the homeless men at our church. We all served in a soup kitchen downtown. We prayed for those we saw on the street.

But they weren't the kids in Haiti.

So when Christmas came around, we gathered toys and personal supplies for needy children. We sent gifts overseas. We gave the shoes off our feet.

But our kids couldn't see the kids they were helping.

They didn't know who they were. They didn't know who their siblings were, couldn't tell what games they liked to play, and certainly never heard anything about them after the holidays.

They wanted more.

They wanted to be a part of another child's life, but not just any child, a child their age to whom they could start to relate on at least some level. They wanted to feel like they were making a difference. They wanted to learn how to put feet to their faith.

After all, isn't that what we all want? Isn't that what Jesus wants for us?

So we didn't wait any longer—not for another tragedy to strike, not for another holiday to come and go, and certainly not until we could get "enough" money.

No way.

Adding to Our Family

We decided to celebrate our daughter's birthday that year by adding to our family.

No, we didn't literally bring a child into our home, but we adopted one into our hearts. Two in fact!

We realized we'd never be able to fully make our kids comprehend the poverty and despair so many of the world's children live with on our own. But what they could relate to was what a child their age thought about and liked to do.

With the help of Compassion International, we were able to locate and sponsor Gabriele in Brazil, who shares Kariss's birthday. As soon as Britton caught wind of what we were doing, he wanted to get in on the giving too; we found a boy with his birthday in India (Ayush).

So what have I learned in the past ten years that has made our child sponsorship experience different this time around?

First, I'm a mom now. The idea of any child hurting absolutely destroys me. And while I still may sometimes make my children feel as if the world revolves around them, I would be doing them a great disservice if I didn't teach them that the very opposite is in fact true: they are each one star in a great big universe. For the galaxy to glow, every person must be present and fully ignited, but though each of us is unique and worthy in the eyes of God, we all shine brighter when we work together.

Second, I know the pictures and letters we receive aren't mass produced in a factory; they are actual images from actual children who greatly look forward to and depend upon our support, prayers, and correspondence. Even though it may seem like we have nothing in common, because our sponsored children are exactly the same ages as our own children, we will always have a connection to what they are going through, dreaming about, and hoping for. That, my friends, is priceless.

Finally, we don't sponsor children because we have to; we sponsor these kids because we want to expand our family in a unique way. While we may not feel called to adopt children into our home at this point, we certainly feel like we have been called to adopt these children into our hearts. And whatever God calls us to, he will equip us for.

Though each of us is unique and worthy in the eyes of God, we all shine brighter when we work together.

Has this been a cure-all to helping our kids understand and fight for the underprivileged children of the world? Far from it. But have our kids included Gabriele and Ayush in their daily prayers and conversations? Absolutely. While they may not have been motivated to learn the native languages of their sponsored siblings, each has expressed interest in actually visiting them one day in their home countries.

Did you catch that? They understand those kids are real. And they want to help them. Before any form of giving can take root in our hearts, we have to wholeheartedly believe in the people or cause to which we are pledging our time, talents, and treasure.

Only time will tell how our family will ultimately change and grow as a result of this experience, but I pray you will feel compelled to consider why you do what you do when it comes to putting feet to your faith as a family. If nothing else, in the process you might learn a little more about who God created you to be.

After all, it's only when we truly know who we are in God's eyes that we can begin to share that gift with others, and I hope you'll be ready and willing to share your own unique giftedness with your kids so they can in turn help others. When you do, I think you'll find that you needed those you help far more than they ever needed you.

A Daily Choice

Child sponsorship is just one of the ways we can encourage our children to demonstrate compassion to the kids of the world. Hopefully by now your kids are beginning to see the ripple effect that can take place by touching just one life around them. When we magnify the principles we've been modeling for them in our home and around town, it only stands to reason that our choices would impact the world as well.

When you started reading this book, you may have been looking for a onetime, surefire way to create more compassion in your children. But compassion isn't a single event; it's a daily choice. Colossians 3:12 tells us to "clothe yourselves with compassion."

Compassion isn't something we simply teach our children. We must put it on each morning and wear it throughout the day. While some argue that the only distinguishing factor between humans and animals is our mental capacity, we carry a distinguishing mark as children of God: compassion.

The Greek word for compassion used in Colossians 3:12 is *oikitrmos*, which literally translates to a "distinguishing mark of a child of God."[2] If God himself is the Father of Compassion (2 Cor. 1:3), then the good news is that as his children, we all have a heart of compassion within us. Some of us just have to dig a little deeper to find it than others.

It's when we doubt ourselves that the Enemy creeps in and gains a foothold in our lives. We begin to believe the lies that we're not good enough, strong enough, or smart enough to do this job called parenting.

Once that lie has some time to sink in, we believe we're too busy, too poor, or too inexperienced to help anyone around us. We start to think our ability to help stems from external factors rather than internal ones. We come up with all the reasons why we can't make a difference rather than coming up with one reason why we can.

Then our kids hear us.

These bright-eyed, open-minded young things who once thought anything was possible start to allow our cynical disbelief to take shape in their hearts.

The same kids who once thought they could sell enough lemonade in a summer to buy a bike turn into teenagers who can't sacrifice texting for a day, much less sacrifice a week of their summer to go on a mission trip overseas.

Unless . . .

They've seen God's love modeled through worship by their parents.

They've found harmony in word and deed in their home.

They've heard gentleness spoken between their parents.

They've learned to bear with their siblings.

They've made things right with those they've wronged.

They've become a light in the darkness at school.

They've stepped into servant leadership in their church community.

They've discovered the needs in their own backyard.

They've lent a hand in their city.

They've allowed peace to rule in their hearts.

They've put feet to their faith in our nation.

They've spoken on behalf of the powerless in this world.

Our goal should not be to raise kids like everyone else in the world; our goal should be to raise our kids in such a way that motivates them to embrace their uniqueness and in turn share that gift with others.

When we as parents take the time to slowly, steadily, and consistently model for our children just how much we can do to make an impact in the lives of others through small, daily choices, we equip them to multiply that effort in their own lives.

While every parent may say they want to raise compassionate kids, the truth is that too few will do what it takes in their own lives to make it happen. To raise uncommon kids, you must be willing to follow uncommon practices.

Our goal should not be to raise kids like everyone else in the world; our goal should be to raise our kids in such a way that motivates them to embrace their uniqueness and in turn share that gift with others. When kids finally internalize that vision, compassion becomes less of a mandate and more of a mission.

! Make It Practical

So you want to change the world? Who doesn't? But by now I pray your idea of changing the world has shifted slightly: instead of imagining a grandiose movement that takes months or even years of planning, I hope you see that changing the world starts with a daily act of the will. Every act of compassion must first begin with submission to God's greater plan in both our lives and the lives of our children.

So what are you waiting for? Grab your kids and take action! Here are a few ideas to get you started:

- *Sponsor a child*: Consider sponsoring a child as a family through organizations like Compassion International or World Vision. Once you sponsor a child, mark your calendar to ensure you continue communication with your child at regular intervals. They love to hear from you as much as you love to hear from them, especially when letters come directly from your kids.
- *Pack a shoe box*: Encourage your children to save their money and then buy items for a shoe box for the Samaritan's Purse

Operation Christmas Child. But don't wait for Christmastime to help—these kids need to hear from us all year long, and believe it or not, shoe boxes are delivered throughout the year too! You can even pack a shoe box online if there isn't a collection going on in your area.

- *Support fair trade*: Begin educating your family about Fair Trade practices. You can support those in need around the world by buying ethically made clothing, accessories, and even food. And if you're shopping for gifts, why not consider buying gifts that also give back? Learn more here: http://samicone.com/shop-to-give-back/.

- *Go on a family mission trip*: Do some research on organizations that lead global mission trips for families. Your best bet is to start by looking into projects or missionary families that your own church supports. If you do sponsor a child, you'll discover those organizations also lead a number of family mission trips throughout the year, and sometimes you can even meet your sponsored child!

- *Work to end human trafficking*: Human trafficking is always a difficult topic to talk about, and depending on the age of your children, you may need to be particularly sensitive about this heartbreaking practice. You can start by joining others in drawing a red X on your hand on Human Trafficking Awareness Day and continue by educating your family and others to look for the signs to prevent this practice from continuing. (Resources are available at HopeForJustice.org and TheA21Campaign.org.)

- *Use social media*: An idea especially good for your teens is to encourage them to use their social media accounts to give a voice and attention to those who cannot speak for themselves. Strides have been made in world issues through social media campaigns, hashtags, and online rallies.

- *Take a Stand*: Encourage your kids to stand up for a cause they love. Share the story of eight-year-old Vivienne Harr who decided to set up a lemonade stand for 365 days, rain or shine, to help end child slavery. She raised $101,320 and sparked a global movement that reminded all of us that you don't have to be big or powerful to change the world. (Learn more at http://stand.tc/.)

For more practical tips and guidelines, visit SamiCone.com/UncommonKids.

BEFORE I GO

I want to share once more the passage that ties together all the truths for raising uncommon kids:

> Therefore, as God's chosen people, holy and dearly loved, clothe yourselves with compassion, kindness, humility, gentleness and patience. Bear with each other and forgive one another if any of you has a grievance against someone. Forgive as the Lord forgave you. And over all these virtues put on love, which binds them all together in perfect unity.
>
> Let the peace of Christ rule in your hearts, since as members of one body you were called to peace. And be thankful. Let the message of Christ dwell among you richly as you teach and admonish one another with all wisdom through psalms, hymns, and songs from the Spirit, singing to God with gratitude in your hearts. And whatever you do, whether in word or deed, do it all in the name of the Lord Jesus, giving thanks to God the Father through him. (Col. 3:12–17)

In chapter five, my spiritual mama, Jackie Kendall, shared a powerful personal lesson on forgiveness. I can't close this book without sharing a story about her, one that transformed my own life.

Jackie and I met shortly after I became a Christian, and she truly epitomized the word *mentor* to me (in fact, she wrote a great book on the topic, *The Mentor Mom*). Whenever possible, she'd invite me to meet with her at her "office" (aka the beach on Singer Island). Even though I'm not a fan of the beach, I welcomed the opportunity to soak up the sun while soaking in Jackie's wisdom and experience.

One such day, I pulled out a notebook and started asking her questions I'd scribbled down during a recent personal quiet time. (Think Yoda and his Jedi trainee, but on the ocean instead of a swamp.) She snatched the notebook out of my hand and asked what exactly it was as she began leafing through it.

"It's just a notebook I keep of thoughts that come to mind as I read my Bible. Sometimes I make note of verses that jump out at me, sometimes I write questions I have about the passages, and other times I write devotions based on what God is teaching me through that day's reading."

She pushed me further. "What are you doing with these thoughts and devotions?"

Under my straw hat, I stared back at her through sunglasses, searching for a better answer. Yet all I could come up with was, "Nothing."

Jackie gave back the notebook, sat up taller in her beach chair, and said something to me I'll never forget as long as I live: "Sami, God does not give us something just to keep it to ourselves. God calls us to be like the Red Sea, not the Dead Sea. If God gives you something, you have to pass it on."

It is with those words that I now challenge you. God has given you a gift in your children, and for one reason or another you were motivated to read this book. Though *Raising Uncommon Kids* is not meant to serve as a step-by-step, how-to guide in raising your children, it is intended to challenge you to ask yourself why you do what you do in your family. With knowledge comes responsibility; now that you have the knowledge, you must pass it on.

May the truth and traits in Colossians 3:12–17 no longer stare at you from the page, presenting a to-do list that seems unachievable. It is my prayer that you and your family now see each of these characteristics and commands for what they are—a love letter from the first parent of all, our heavenly Father, who longs to share his heart with us so we may in turn share it with others.

The best way to exponentially share this love letter with the world is by first sharing it with our own children. May you move forward like the Red Sea in raising uncommon kids.

ACKNOWLEDGMENTS

For some reason, this feels a bit like writing an acceptance speech, except that instead of me holding a golden statue, I hope to turn the lens on all the deserving people who helped make this God wink a reality.

First and foremost, I need to thank God. In the midst of one of the lowest and most uncertain points in my life, the only thing you made clear was the message in this book. Thank you for always having your hand on me, even when I was too blind to see it or too busy to feel it.

Ricky, you are my husband, the father of our children, and my partner forever. We've been gifted in such different ways, and yet you encourage me to pursue my passions even when you don't understand them. Thank you for fighting for us.

To my firstborn, Kariss Nevaeh, my muse for this book—you are the mirror through which I learn each and every day. I always say you are a better version of me and your contribution to this project proves that.

To my one and only son, Britton Jerick—thank you for always believing I'm capable of more than I think. I love who I look like through your eyes, and your unconditional love and generosity inspire and encourage me daily.

My parents instilled in me from an early age that I could accomplish whatever I set my mind to, laying a foundation for being uncommon in my own life. Thank you, Mom, Dawn Strauss, for *always* being there for me, even when I didn't know what I wanted or needed. Thank you, Dad, Jerry Strauss, for teaching me not to be afraid of hard work or naysayers.

While she prefers to stay behind the scenes, my BFF Carolyn Master is always front and center in my life. You balance me so well, friend, and I'm ever grateful for your wisdom and experience beyond your years.

This book would never have come to life without some key friends:

Lindsey Nobles: Your willingness to listen to my heart over chicken salad at Frothy Monkey and let me share my story with a friend will never be forgotten.

Bob Goff: Thank you for picking up the phone and telling me to shoot for the stars.

Don Jacobson: You're so much more than an agent. I'm grateful for you as a friend and mentor—and the fact that you were willing to split an omelet the first time we met proved that this partnership was going to work. Thank you for seeing how this book needed to take shape before I could.

Annie Downs: You took what was in my head and so eloquently helped me organize it on more colored Post-it notes than I've ever seen in one sitting. Thank you for not keeping your gift all to yourself (and for being my loud-laughing sister who still finds me funny).

Jeremy, Tiffany, Solomon, Oliver, and Clementine Lee: You epitomize "chosen family," and I'm so grateful we get to do life together!

A wealth of gratitude is owed to the precious mentoring moms who contributed their parenting wisdom to these pages: Donna

Mullins, Jane Randlett, Diana Sumpter, Catherine Hickem, Jackie Kendall, Barbara Rainey, Tricia Goyer, Cindy Easley, Barbara Cameron, Tracey Eyster, Reese Dixon, and Dawn Strauss.

I owe extra special thanks to the mentor who has consistently been there to answer my questions and model what the Titus 2 woman looks like: my spiritual mama, Jackie Kendall.

I also want to thank the team at D.C. Jacobson & Associates, especially Blair and Marty, for patiently walking with me through this journey.

Finally, thanks to the team at Baker Books for birthing this baby with me, especially Rebekah, who caught the vision from the get-go; Jamie, who edited this manuscript countless times; Wendy, who helped bring clarity; and Ruth, who put up with my endless ideas.

And to each and every one of you who decided to pick up this book, thank you! Whether it's because you wanted to support me or simply liked the cover; whether it's because you felt hopeful or hopeless in your parenting—I'm grateful that you took the time to invest in the most important job you'll ever have.

NOTES

Introduction

1. Dr. Henry Cloud and Dr. John Townsend, *Boundaries with Kids* (Grand Rapids: Zondervan, 1998).

Chapter 1: Love—Above All Else

1. Interview with Donna Mullins, April 17, 2015.

Chapter 2: Harmony—Lessons Are Caught

1. Oswald Chambers, *My Utmost for His Highest* (Grand Rapids: Discovery House, 1992), June 25.
2. Interview with Jane Randlett, April 10, 2015.
3. Patrick Lencioni, *The 3 Big Questions for a Frantic Family* (San Francisco: Jossey Bass, 2008).
4. Myquillyn Smith, *The Nesting Place* (Grand Rapids: Zondervan, 2014).

Chapter 3: Gentleness—Be Careful, Little Ears, What You Hear

1. Walter A. Elwell, ed., *Evangelical Dictionary of Biblical Theology* (Grand Rapids: Baker Books, 1996), 286.
2. Interview with Diana Sumpter, April 11, 2015.
3. John Piper, *The Power of Words and the Wonder of God* (Wheaton: Crossway, 2009), 80.
4. Jim Stovall, *The Ultimate Gift: A Novel* (Colorado Springs: David C. Cook, 2001).

Chapter 4: Bearing With—The Secret of Sibling Love

1. Alan Abrahamson, "Giving up a Spot in the Games," 3WireSports.com, January 13, 2014, http://www.3wiresports.com/2014/01/13/giving-spot-olympics/.
2. Gary Chapman and Ross Campbell, *The 5 Love Languages of Children* (Chicago: Moody, 1997).
3. Interview with Catherine Hickem, April 15, 2015.

Section Two: Your Attitude toward Others

1. Joyce Meyer, *Enjoying Everyday Life*, podcast audio, accessed February 2, 2015, http://www.joycemeyer.org/BroadcastHome.aspx?video=The_Power_of_Words_-_Part_1.

Chapter 5: Forgiveness—Respect What Your Kids Need to Know

1. Celebrate Recovery is "a biblical and balanced program that helps us overcome our hurts, hang-ups, and habits." For more information, visit http://www.celebraterecovery.com/.
2. John Maxwell, *Failing Forward: Turning Mistakes into Stepping Stones for Success* (Nashville: Thomas Nelson, 2007), 5.
3. Dr. Henry Cloud and Dr. John Townsend, *Boundaries: When to Say Yes, How to Say No to Take Control of Your Life* (Grand Rapids: Zondervan, 1992), 48, emphasis added.
4. Oswald Chambers, *My Utmost for His Highest* (Grand Rapids: Discovery House, 1992), June 27.
5. Interview with Jackie Kendall, April 7, 2015.

Chapter 6: Wisdom—Through the Eyes of a Child

1. Spiros Zodhiates, *Hebrew-Greek Key Word Study Bible* (Chattanooga, TN: AMG Publishers, 1997), 736–39.
2. Ibid., 736.
3. Ron Hall and Denver Moore, *Same Kind of Different As Me: A Modern-Day Slave, an International Art Dealer, and the Unlikely Woman Who Bound Them Together* (Nashville: Thomas Nelson, 2009), 235.
4. Interview with Barbara Rainey, April 15, 2015.

Chapter 7: Patience—Active Restraint

1. Bill Hybels, *Too Busy Not to Pray* (Westmont, IL: InterVarsity, 1988), 23.
2. Interview with Tricia Goyer, April 29, 2015.
3. Richard A. Swenson, *Margin: Restoring Emotional, Physical, Financial, and Time Reserves to Overloaded Lives* (Carol Stream, IL: NavPress, 2014), back cover.
4. Lance Witt, *Replenish: Leading from a Healthy Soul* (Grand Rapids: Baker Books, 2011), 163–66.

Chapter 8: Kindness—The Need Next Door

1. Spiros Zodhiates, *Hebrew-Greek Key Word Study Bible* (Chattanooga, TN: AMG Publishers, 1997), 1663.
2. Interview with Cindy Easley, April 7, 2015.

Section Three: Your Influence in the World

1. Oxford Dictionaries, *influence*, http://www.oxforddictionaries.com/us/defi nition/american_english/influence.

Chapter 9: Gratitude—Kids Can Too

1. Stephanie Hamlow, "Volunteering: Service Brings Gratitude, Happiness, Appreciation, Love," BuildingBridgesForWomenInBusiness.com, May 8, 2014, http://buildingbridgesforwomeninbusiness.com/volunteering-service-brings -gratitude-happiness-appreciation-love/.
2. *My Big Fat Greek Wedding*, Gold Circle Films, 2002.
3. Spiros Zodhiates, *Hebrew-Greek Key Word Study Bible* (Chattanooga, TN: AMG Publishers, 1997), 1561.
4. Jeffrey Froh and Giacomo Bono, "Seven Ways to Foster Gratitude in Kids," GreaterGood.Berkeley.edu, March 5, 2014, http://greatergood.berkeley.edu/article/ item/seven_ways_to_foster_gratitude_in_kids.
5. Interview with Barbara Cameron, April 5, 2015.

Chapter 10: Peace—Option Z

1. Oswald Chambers, *My Utmost for His Highest* (Grand Rapids: Discovery House, 1992), January 1.
2. Corrie ten Boom, *Reflections of God's Glory* (Grand Rapids: Zondervan, 1999), 39.
3. Eleanor Roosevelt, *Quotations by Eleanor Roosevelt*, http://www.gwu. edu/~erpapers/, March 3, 2015, http://www.gwu.edu/~erpapers/abouteleanor/ er-quotes/.
4. Interview with Tracey Eyster, April 30, 2015.
5. Spiros Zodhiates, *Hebrew-Greek Key Word Study Bible* (Chattanooga, TN: AMG Publishers, 1997), 1615.
6. Dallas Willard, *Willard Words*, dwillard.org, March 17, 2015, http://www. dwillard.org/resources/WillardWords.asp

Chapter 11: Humility—Consider Others

1. Dale Carnegie, *How to Win Friends and Influence People* (New York: Simon & Schuster, 2010), 109.
2. Interview with Reese Dixon, April 28, 2015.

Chapter 12: Compassion—Both/And

1. Interview with Dawn P. Strauss, April 30, 2015.
2. Spiros Zodhiates, *Hebrew-Greek Key Word Study Bible* (Chattanooga, TN: AMG Publishers, 1997), 1665.

Sami Cone is a blogger (SamiCone.com), radio host, and TV correspondent mentoring others to live their dream life on less and pursue their passions. She draws on her experiences as a writer, editor, university professor, performer, professional athlete, and pageant winner to help people realize their full potential in life. Sami is known as the "Frugal Mom" on Nashville's top-rated TV talk show *Talk of the Town*, hosts the nationally syndicated radio program *Family Money Minute*, and educates over a million listeners on radio's *Family Friendly Morning Show*. She is proud to call Nashville home with her husband, Rick, and their two children, Kariss and Britton.

FOLLOW THE AUTHOR

sami

SAMICONE.COM

   @TheSamiCone SamiCone samaracone

family money MINUTE *with Sami Cone*

Family Money Minute is a 60-second nationally syndicated program designed to help families maximize their money today so they make more memories tomorrow! Savings expert, blogger, and media personality Sami Cone takes two of the hottest topics affecting our day-to-day living, family and money, and combines them into practical tidbits that anyone can use to immediately impact their lives.

FamilyMoneyMinute.com